Those were the days ...™

British

Drag Racing

The early years

Nicholas Pettitt

VELOCE PUBLISHING
THE PUBLISHER OF FINE AUTOMOTIVE BOOKS

Also from Veloce –

Those Were The Days ... Series
Alpine Trials & Rallies 1910-1973 (Pfundner)
American 'Independent' Automakers – AMC to Willys 1945 to 1960 (Mort)
American Station Wagons – The Golden Era 1950-1975 (Mort)
American Trucks of the 1950s (Mort)
American Trucks of the 1960s (Mort)
American Woodies 1928-1953 (Mort)
Anglo-American Cars from the 1930s to the 1970s (Mort)
Austerity Motoring (Bobbitt)
Austins, The last real (Peck)
Brighton National Speed Trials (Gardiner)
British Drag Racing – The Early Years (Pettitt)
British Lorries of the 1950s (Bobbitt)
British Lorries of the 1960s (Bobbitt)
British Touring Car Racing (Collins)
British Police Cars (Walker)
British Woodies (Peck)
Café Racer Phenomenon, The (Walker)
Drag Bike Racing in Britain – From the mid '60s to the mid '80s (Lee)
Dune Buggy Phenomenon, The (Hale)
Dune Buggy Phenomenon Volume 2, The (Hale)
Endurance Racing at Silverstone in the 1970s & 1980s (Parker)
Hot Rod & Stock Car Racing in Britain in the 1980s (Neil)
Last Real Austins 1946-1959, The (Peck)
MG's Abingdon Factory (Moylan)
Motor Racing at Brands Hatch in the Seventies (Parker)
Motor Racing at Brands Hatch in the Eighties (Parker)
Motor Racing at Crystal Palace (Collins)
Motor Racing at Goodwood in the Sixties (Gardiner)
Motor Racing at Nassau in the 1950s & 1960s (O'Neil)
Motor Racing at Oulton Park in the 1960s (McFadyen)
Motor Racing at Oulton Park in the 1970s (McFadyen)
Superprix – The Story of Birmingham Motor Race (Page & Collins)
Three Wheelers (Bobbitt)

From Veloce Publishing's new imprints –

BATTLE CRY!

Soviet General & field rank officer uniforms: 1955 to 1991 (Streather)
Red & Soviet military & paramilitary services: female uniforms 1941-1991 (Streather)

Hubble & Hattie

Animal Grief (Alderton)
Bramble: the dog who wanted to live forever (Heritage)
Clever Dog! (O'Meara)
Complete Dog Massage Manual, The – Gentle Dog Care (Robertson)
Dinner with Rover (Paton-Ayre)
Dog Cookies (Schops)
Dog Games – stimulating play to entertain your dog and you (Blenski)
Dog Relax – Relaxed dogs, relaxed owners (Pilguj)
Dogs on wheels (Mort)
Exercising your puppy: a gentle & natural approach (Robertson)
Fun and games for cats! (Seidl)
Know Your Dog – The guide to a beautiful relationship (Birmelin)
Living with an Older Dog – Gentle Dog Care (Alderton & Hall)
Walking the dog – motorway walks for drivers and dogs (Rees)
My dog has cruciate ligament injury (Hausler)
My dog has hip dysplasia (Hausler)
My dog is blind – but lives life to the full! (Horsky)
My dog is deaf (Willms)
Smellorama – nose games for dogs (Theby)
Swim to recovery: Canine hydrotherapy healing (Wong)
Waggy Tails & Wheelchairs (Epp)
Winston ... the dog who changed my life (Klute)
You and Your Border Terrier – The Essential Guide (Alderton)
You and Your Cockapoo – The Essential Guide (Alderton)

www.veloce.co.uk

First published in March 2011 by Veloce Publishing Limited, Veloce House, Parkway Farm Business Park, Middle Farm Way, Poundbury, Dorchester, Dorset, DT1 3AR, England.
Fax 01305 250479/e-mail info@veloce.co.uk/web www.veloce.co.uk or www.velocebooks.com.
ISBN: 978-1-845843-37-3 UPC: 6-36847-04337-7

Readers with ideas for automotive books, or books on other transport or related hobby subjects, are invited to write to the editorial director of Veloce Publishing at the above address.
British Library Cataloguing in Publication Data – A catalogue record for this book is available from the British Library. Typesetting, design and page make-up all by Veloce Publishing Ltd on Apple Mac. Printed in India by Imprint Digital.

Contents

Acknowledgements

The author is greatly indebted to the following for their help with the book:

Mike Collins, who not only wrote many of the features in *Drag Racing & Hot Rod Magazine*, and other publications which have proved invaluable in the author's research, but spent countless hours with the author adding a few of his own ideas, words, and memories from the 1960s when he was a writer, photographer, commentator, Santa Pod PR man and racer.

Also Brian Sparrow, who organised some of the first British Drag races, formed Dragster Developments with pioneer racer Allan Herridge, and contributed to *Drag Racing & Hot Rod Magazine* with his comprehensive *Scene in the pits* reports. Brian made available to the author his huge British drag racing archive.

Thanks must also go to John Bennett and Bob Phelps, who gave British Drag Racing a permanent venue with Santa Pod Raceway. John also took many of the black and white photographs credited to Mike Collins Archives for Drag Racing & Hot Rod Magazine, and Mike has made these rare photos available to the author. The photographers of some images taken from Mike Collins Archives are unknown.

The author and his Ford Popular Gasser. (Courtesy Mike Collins)

40 years on and Mike Collins finds nitro nirvana on the start line with the 2008 US Drag Team during the UK's first Cacklefest at Goodwood. (Courtesy Andy Willsheer)

Introduction

Racing 'against the clock' amongst the wealthy has been going on since the motor car first arrived on the scene. However, shortly after the second World War ended in 1945, the West Coast of America saw the rise of a new breed of racers interested in straight-line acceleration. It also saw the birth of a new sport. Initially born on the streets, as returning US servicemen, bored with the aged automobiles available, began to 'hop-up' their machines.

A growing speed equipment market saw Robert Petersen and long-time SCTA man Wally Parks launch *Hot Rod Magazine* in 1948 at the first Hot Rod show put together by Petersen in Los Angeles.

This new breed of racers was more interested in 'go' than 'show,' and had little time for the wide open spaces of the dry lakes used for so long by the prewar hot rodders. Wild machines were raced from red light to red light, and they called it 'drag racing.' Eventually things became organized, and the first 'legal' drag race took place near Goleta in April 1949 when a stretch of highway was closed off by the police in order for folks to race with a modicum of safety. On Sunday June 19th 1950 the legendary CJ Hart opened the first commercial dragstrip at Santa Ana, California with great success.

This exciting new sport grew like wildfire during the next decade and drag racing over a standing start quarter-mile was soon the norm. The search began for shorter elapsed times and faster speeds, and it wasn't long before basic and often 'agricultural' machines began to become more sophisticated. Racers realised that more was required than just a fast car. Sure, you had to have power, but, unlike sprinting, drag racers faced an opponent, so the driver required good reactions. Most important of all, you needed traction, the ability to get power to the ground. The most effective

When editor Wally Parks founded the National Hot Rod Association in 1951, *Hot Rod Magazine* became the drag racer's bible and was responsible for spreading the 'word' throughout the USA and beyond.

• *President of the "There's no substitute for inches" Club of the World, Jones sits in the mouth of self-created monster, still a bit apprehensive.*

BRITAIN'S FASTEST DRAGSTER?

Imagine mating a Hawker airplane with an armoured car! That's just what Ted Lloyd-Jones of Birmingham, England, did. The result turned out to be the most powerful sprint and hill-climb special in Britain today. Starting with model making, Ted has worked his way up from where at 17 he made his first runabout – a three-wheeler with a wheel width narrow enough to be able to park it in the parlor – to this latest bomb that has yet to have its ultimate maximum speed recorded. Through the years dozens of others have been built or modified and this experience has meant that nothing on wheels is impossible to this engineering genius. When he saw a V12-cylinder Rolls Royce Kestrel engine for sale as war surplus, it was only natural for him to buy it. He had no idea that he would ever use it, but it seemed a pity that such a fine engine should rust away on a dump. After that it was only a matter of time before the idea of building it into a car began to weigh upon him.

dragster layout was the 'slingshot,' which had the driver sitting behind the rear axle and the engine in front, producing a static weight distribution of 90 per cent on the rear tyres, or 100 per cent under acceleration.

More than just spreading the word, *Hot Rod Magazine* was also mindful of the British straight-line scene. The December 1953 issue not only carried the banner 'Britain builds a DRAGSTER,' it had a three-page feature on Birmingham's Ted Lloyd-Jones and his huge 21-litre V12 Rolls-Royce Kestrel-powered beast.

Autosport's July 1955 issue carried a photo and the following caption: "John Nybert's supercharged Thunderbird in the drag meeting held last Sunday at Shepherds Grove USAF base." Already, US servicemen were indulging in their favourite past-time while on duty in the UK.

Hot Rod Magazine featured Ted Lloyd-Jones' V12 British sprinter in 1953, calling it a dragster, but sprinting was still the name of the game in the UK, and it would be some time before Brits went the quarter-mile drag racing route.

Warming up 1960-1965

September 1960 saw the birth of the British Hot Rod Association (BHRA) following a joint meeting of hot rod clubs from the Uxbridge area. Brian Coole and American hot rodder Lee Siebenthaler laid the groundwork for the Association, later joined by Vic Outen, who began the long and laborious task of educating the British public about the excitement drag racing offered with countless letters to the motoring press.

Meanwhile, a broad-framed, quiet-spoken, bespectacled south London gentleman was looking for a fresh challenge. As proprietor of the Allard Motor Company, 51-year-old Sydney Allard was well-known in motorsport, having triumphed in sprinting, hill climbing, endurance racing, and winning the prestigious Monte Carlo Rally in 1952. Sydney was also a hot rodding pioneer and had a loving and prosperous relationship with American horsepower in his legendary Allard J2 sports cars. These long-nosed beasts, with motivation from flathead Fords through early hemi Mopars to mighty Cadillacs, were real hot rods, built to provide amazing motoring thrills for speed fanatics with deep pockets.

Allards found their way to the drag strip in America. This J2 ran well in the 1950s in Allentown, Pennsylvania. (Courtesy Martyn Schorr)

Chris Karamesines in his 200mph Chizler dragster from *Best Hot Rods 1960*, probably the publication that inspired Sydney Allard.

Sydney's Allard Chrysler dragster helped kick-start British drag racing in 1961. (Courtesy Freddie Grevett)

While leafing through an American hot rodding magazine, Sydney found instant inspiration in the exploits of Chris Karamesines and his Chizler dragster, which had just clocked 200mph in the standing start quarter-mile, something mathematicians at the time believed was physically impossible. Arriving at work the next day Sydney exclaimed: "Let's build one of these," as he slammed the magazine down on the desk.

Work began in January 1961 on a dragster designed by Dave Hooper at Allards with a Hilborn-injected blown 354in^3 Chrysler Hemi for power. RAC regulations did not have a dragster class so it was deemed a racing car, requiring a full engine cover and front brakes. This rule in turn led to the choice of a front-mounted Potvin blower and the beautiful and very swoopy aluminium body panels.

Brian Witty's low buck machine lacked the beauty of the Allard Chrysler dragster, but it did inspire other hot rodders to have a go. (Courtesy Brian Sparrow)

By July 1961, the team led by John Hume had finished building the Allard Chrysler dragster, and it was ready to make some noise in a static display at Brands Hatch. Then, following trial runs on the Silverstone Club straight, they entered the Allard in the Brighton Speed Trials, but teething problems kept the team from showing its true potential.

Early in 1962 the National Sprint Association (NSA) invited the BHRA to its 'Noggin and Natter' meetings to discuss the possibilities of four-wheel drag racing in Britain with RAC sanctioning. Brian Sparrow was competitions secretary of the NSA, which had been organising bike sprints since 1958, and it was at one of these meetings that Brian met BHRA members Allan Herridge and Brian Witty, who were already building dragsters. Not everyone had the budget and facilities available to Allard. These two were basic hot rodders, taking their dreams from the pages of *Hot Rod* and building them to the best of their ability and limited funds. Herridge was working on a straight-eight Buick-powered device, and Witty on a Chrysler hemi-powered slingshot, both with plans to compete against Sydney Allard at the annual Long Marston Sprint in June. These were ambitious plans because, by now, Sydney had driven the Allard Chrysler to a 10.48s elapsed time at Debden. By June, Witty had finished his dragster, and Brian Sparrow joined the team for its trip to Long Marston. However, despite help from the Allard boys, the Witty dragster just would not run, let alone make it to the line.

While Allard, Herridge, and Witty were going the large American engine route, Tony Densham and Harry Worrall had come up with the idea of using a small British engine in a lighter frame as a recipe for a competitive dragster, using a 1500cc Ford motor and Shorrock blower. They built a tube chassis and had it ready to enter Sprint meetings in 1963.

Herridge's dragster was now progressing under the banner of Dragster Developments, a syndicate formed to provide a much needed cash injection. It consisted of

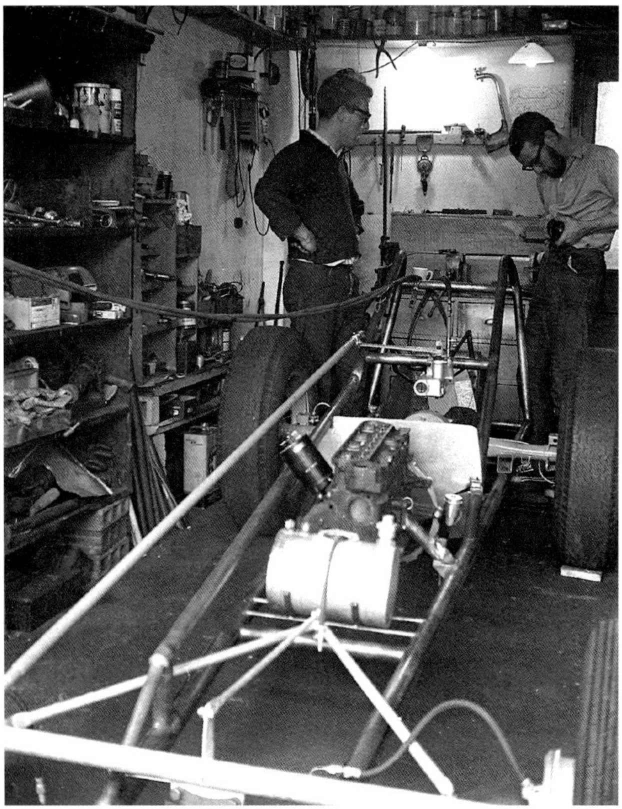

Tony Densham and Harry Worrall built their dragster, Worden, on American lines, but with a small British engine and drive train. (Courtesy www.oldstox.com)

Allan Herridge's first dragster, straight-eight Buick-powered, and later fitted with a front-mounted supercharger. (Courtesy Brian Sparrow)

Brian Sparrow, John Harrison, Robin Evemy, and Allan Herridge, and preparations were soon moving ahead for the 1963 season. Most of the work on this pioneering dragster was being done at Robin's mum's house as it had the luxury of a lock-up garage. The workmanship was already showing a quality which would later become an Allan Herridge trademark.

The Dragster Developments Buick made its debut at the West Essex Car Club Sprint at Debden in March 1963 with Allan Herridge running a best of 16.68s. After

September 1963 saw the arrival of Mooneyes, the first American dragster on British soil. (Courtesy Mike Collins Archives)

some modifications, the team improved to 14.23s at Long Marston in June, its best run for that year.

Following *Hot Rod Magazine*'s failure to bring Calvin Rice's nitro-burning dragster to the 1958 Brighton Speed Trials due to international unrest, there had been endless correspondence between automobile organisations in the USA and England concerning similar ventures, but with no success. Things changed when Dante Duce, a young Las Vegas speed shop owner, managed to break through the red tape. He took matters into his own hands and simply placed an overseas phone call to Allard himself on July 23rd, challenging him to a match race in England. An invitation followed, and Duce persuaded Dean Moon and team to join him, along with the beautiful Mooneyes supercharged, petrol-burning Chevy-powered dragster. The fact that Duce had driven it to 10.29s and 147mph on its debut in 1961 no doubt helped.

The tour began with a demonstration for the press and VIPs using Silverstone's Club straight on Tuesday 10th September. The cars ran together a couple of times but Allard could not better 13.81s, and with Mooneyes running 4.40 gears its performance was not exactly earth shattering. However, for the last run of the day the Mooneyes team swapped in a set of drag racers' 4.11 gears and fitted fresh slicks. It worked, and Dante Duce blasted off the line to run the quickest and fastest quarter-mile outside the USA – recording the first single digit elapsed time of 9.48s at 167mph! Famed motor racing journalist and competitor Denis 'Jenks' Jenkinson witnessed this from the start line and was particularly impressed with what he saw, later writing in *Motor Sport* magazine that: "It was the most shattering and exciting thing that I have seen for quite a long time, the noise and smoke from the tyres being more than a whole Grand Prix field can put together at a start. The black marks on the track ran for two-thirds of the measured quarter-mile."

Drag racing's smoke and thunder had arrived, and the Mooneyes team had left its mark.

The Brighton Speed Trials was where Allard and Duce were due to take part in a match race. Drag racing legend Mickey Thompson had taken everyone by surprise when he turned up completely unannounced with his dragster, the Harvey Aluminum Special, courtesy of the US Air Force. More than that though, Thompson's 427in^3 Ford-powered machine was a genuine AA/Fuel Dragster; that's supercharged, fuel-injected and running nitro! Thompson joined the challenge at Brighton and became an instant thorn in the officials' sides, informing them they were "doin' it all wrong" with reference to their archaic staging procedures.

On the day, RAC officials restricted the dragsters to short blasts along Madeira Drive, yet these were sufficient to completely blow the minds of the British spectators and many new drag fans were made that sunny day on Brighton seafront.

The following week the tour moved to Church Lawford where times were down as the strip was more than just bumpy; it was reported that moss grew from some of the joints in the surface, not exactly conducive to high speeds and M&H slicks! The lightweight Mooneyes ran 13.25s at 115mph, while the heavier Allard sped to 127mph in 11.34s. Mickey Thompson also ran, thrilling fans each time he fired up, yet could only muster 10.64s at 141mph.

The track at Debden the next day was vastly superior. Although, like all NSA sprint meetings, it was a ticket only event, around five thousand fans reportedly managed to talk their way in, and what a show they got. Wowed by the smoke and wheelstanding antics of Mooneyes, they found themselves almost wilting as the Harvey Aluminum Special was fired up. Thompson had added some nitro to the tank, or as drag aficionados would say 'tipped the can,' and for the first time UK fans learned the true meaning of nitro power. The ground shook and the air came strong with nitro fumes as the silver machine took off, thundering down the track ahead of a wall of tyre smoke to record the quickest and fastest quarter-mile outside of the USA; 178mph in 8.84s!

Shortly after an announcement that the two American dragsters were going to race fans were thronging the track, or at least as close as they could get. Dean Moon handled the flag start and Dante Duce smoked off the line. Moments later, Mickey Thompson unleashed the power and fury of his AA/Fuel Dragster hard off the line, soon passing Duce and leaving Mooneyes in the distance.

The media enjoyed the spectacle of real drag racing. This shot from *The Motor* clearly shows Duce's car length holeshot on Thompson at Debden.

The Motor magazine reported: "Duce got away first in a cloud of blue tyre smoke, front wheels clawing the air, but Thompson took off in pursuit and by halfway had caught and passed his rival." The report continued: "Then Thompson's Harvey Aluminum Special veered to the left in front of Duce's Mooneyes blinding the pilot with smoke from the still spinning tyres. Duce veered off course and had to pull the ripcord of his parachute to slow enough to be able to steer through the finishing gate."

Even then, Mickey Thompson was a genuine hot rodding outlaw, and expressed the desire to make a run at the 250mph barrier in the half-mile. Following his earlier smoke down, such a run was deemed "suicidal" by RAC stewards, who replied in a single syllable: "No!"

Although the Americans had only made a couple of power blasts at Brighton, and only a few quarter-mile passes in front of spectators, their visit received tremendous coverage. It left fans clamouring for more, arming Sydney Allard with the knowledge that the future of British drag racing lay in making such a spectacle available to a larger audience.

To this end, the '1st British International Drag Festival' was announced at a press conference in London's Kensington Palace Hotel on Tuesday 7th January. The six-race series was to be held at venues

Garlits' new-style upswept 'zoomie' headers blew the tyre smoke off the tyres, while Ivo enjoyed blasting away past eager photographers with his noisier 'weed burners.' These awe-inspiring AA/Fuel Dragsters raced at the end of each day during the 1964 Drag Festivals, leaving the fans buzzing. (Courtesy Brian Sparrow)

around England over three weekends from the 19th September, featuring top American dragsters and bikes. The British Drag Racing Association (BDRA) was formed in June to run the festival with Sydney Allard as president, Gerry Belton as secretary, and NHRA's Wally Parks also on the board.

The Dragster Developments team was now in business; advertising dragster frames and parts for sale late in the 1963 season based on the components used in its DD Buick dragster, now running a blower. The team was also building a lightweight slingshot with A90 Austin Atlantic power for John Harrison.

On a different scale, Allards was busy designing and building a pair of Shorrock supercharged 1500cc Ford-powered dragsters for 1964 with smaller, lighter chassis based loosely on the big Allard. These would be called Allard Dragons, which it planned to sell in kit form along with its own brand 'Dragstar' components.

Meanwhile, the BHRA was ready to run the first British drag race meeting. An earlier attempt in August 1963 had been cancelled due to a lack of entries. This time, thanks to co-promotion with the Allard Owners Club and the NSA, 57 eager competitors turned up at Duxford airfield for the 'Big Go' on Whit Sunday May 17th.

The sun shone, fans were seen sporting T-shirts emblazoned with Moon and Dragstar logos, and the track even had 'Christmas tree' countdown start lights provided by club secretary Peter Bartlett. Cars ran class eliminations as well as Top, Middle, and Little Eliminator where the field was split into three performance brackets irrespective of class. Some entrants who did not follow American drag racing were a bit taken aback by this, but there were some interesting and close races. Naturally, the Allard Dragons performed well, and Gerry Belton won Top Eliminator in his Dragon while John Hume ran 11.92s to take low elapsed time in the Works Dragon. The meeting was completed by 6pm, everyone went home happy, even the RAC Steward enjoyed the days racing, and much was learnt by club officials about the running of a drag race meeting.

The International Drag Festival was set to kick off at Blackbushe airport, then on to the RAF bases at Chelveston, Woodvale, Church Fenton, and Kemble, ending up back at Blackbushe for the final round. The two nitro-burning AA/Fuel Dragsters of Don Garlits and Tommy Ivo gave fans an unprecedented glimpse of ground pounding thunder with side-by-side low

Despite the appearance of stock automobiles, the amazing A/FX cars stood tall, the drivers' four-speed power shifting sounding like automatic transmissions. (Courtesy Brian Sparrow)

K S Pittman's Willys broke its rear axle, therefore missing the first few rounds when his spare parts container was mislaid for several days at Southampton docks. (Courtesy Brian Sparrow)

BHRA's Peter Bartlett used his Shovin' Chevy to push-start the American dragsters, seen here with Doug Church's Porsche dragster. (Courtesy Brian Sparrow)

Talk about a spacious cabin! Houndog takes off with tyres spinning at Blackbushe. The staging chock harks back to early sprinting days. (Courtesy Brian Sparrow)

eight-second races, leaving the quarter-mile covered in walls of tyre smoke.

During an interview with Mike Collins some years later, Don Garlits commented: "We just match raced at a lot of different strips and we barely touched the two hundred (mph) mark. I think I ran a hundred and ninety seven as top speed, we ran about eighty-five per cent nitro and the cars were push-started ... we didn't do burnouts, we just went straight up to the line, made the run and the tyres smoked right on through the lights."

NHRA President Wally Parks found the British machines interesting, not least Clive Waye's unique, super-long slingshot bike. (Courtesy Brian Sparrow)

Sydney Allard stands proud, as son Alan lights up the slicks for the last time in the Allard Chrysler at Blackbushe in 1964. The dragster was brought out of retirement for a full restoration by the 'Allard Chrysler Action Group' in 2008. (Courtesy Mike Collins Archives)

Obviously the AA/Fuel Dragsters were the big crowd favourites, but the pair of supercharged 1933 Willys Gassers of George Montgomery and KS Pittman, which seemingly bounced their way to ten-second times at over 145mph, thrilled fans in a different way, as did Ronnie Sox and Dave Strickler, who match raced their mighty 11-second Factory Experimentals.

Doug Church's Porsche-powered machine was the one American dragster that stood a chance of being beaten by a British car, and Alan Allard did just that in the works Allard Dragon. Bob Keith drove Dos Palmos, a blown and injected gas-burning Chevy, that thrilled fans with smoky wheelstanding nine-second passes. Tony Nancy's radical new rear-engined Wedge II looked good, ran strong, but was getting out of shape at the top end. He had an expensive visit, venting no less than three Plymouth blocks while his 22 Jr slingshot was pranged by Dante Duce who rolled it at Chelveston.

An intrepid Alan Burgess made some shakedown runs at Blackbushe on his twin Turbonique rocket-powered go-kart. (Courtesy Brian Sparrow)

Duce did a better job in the blown Chevy-powered Moonbeam sports car, clocking low 11s, and he also had a few close match-ups with some of the British sports cars in his Shelby Cobra.

Two American drag bikes came over, Don Hyland's twin Triumph and Bill Wood's Harley, and they both entered eliminations with the British bikes.

Nobby Hills turned up with Houndog, based on the Allard dragster but using Jaguar power and a small Marshall blower. Les Hill drove it to 14.46s at 83mph. Leon Moss and Syd Marston's Square One dragster had a Shorrock blown 1500cc prewar Riley that took it to 14.07s and 91mph. More than just new, Derek Metcalfe's 2-litre Triumph TR2 dragster Wombat had Allan Herridge helping set up the steering geometry. Denis Jenkinson drove Gerry Belton's Dragon, which had some competition from Tony Densham, whose Worden ran a best of 11.55s at 120mph. Alan Allard dragged out the ageing Allard Chrysler for its last blasts down the quarter-mile before retirement, and at the final

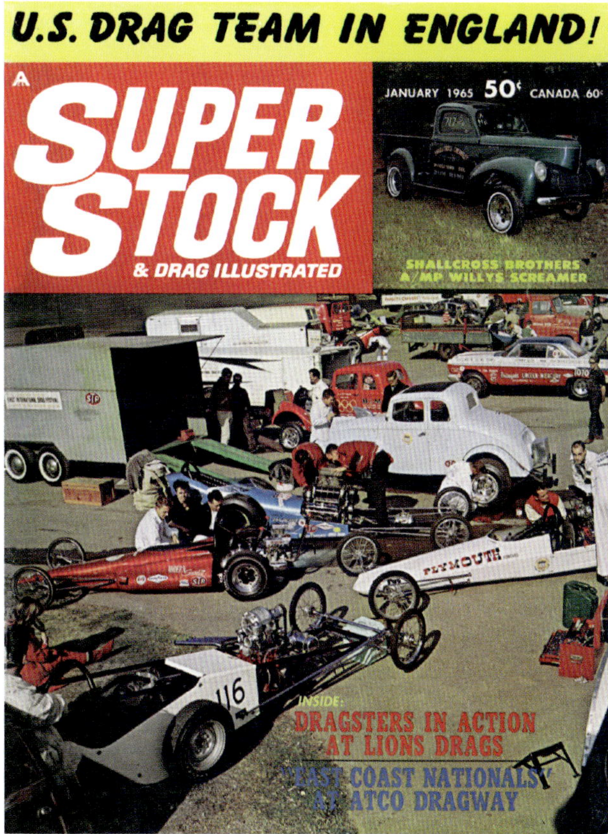

Jim Kelly, *SSDI's* ace photographer, came with the US team for the 1964 Drag Festivals, and this much prized January edition, which contained a 16-page tour feature, justified the expense.

meet he got the slicks smoking to a best-ever 10.28s. John Harrison couldn't quite get in the 14s with the DD Atlantic and ran a best of 15.07s. Herridge got down to 13.41s at 98mph before adding some nitro to the tank at the last meeting, which meant a 12s run or bust – unfortunately, he bust!

The BDRA began running monthly practice days at Graveley in 1965, and a drag race at Swindon in July, while the BHRA ran its '2nd Big Go' at Duxford in June.

The Dragster Developments team brought out a new Cadillac V8 dragster, and the DD Atlantic now had a lighter chassis. Tony Densham also had a new chassis for the Worden, and Nobby Hills had built a new super-long Houndog II; Jag-powered again, its bigger Wade blower soon put the team in the low 12s.

Ken Cooper finally made it out with his Ford flathead V8 dragster. He had begun in 1962 with a frame and axles, but the RAC regulations requiring front brakes and covered engine put him off so he built a 1933 Ford hot rod instead. When the regs were changed he literally dragged it out of the weeds in his garden to finish it off.

From Wales came a slingshot called Dafydd 1, built on a Ford Popular chassis with flathead V8 power. Dave Price entered it at the Big Go but it didn't get past scrutineering and was never seen again.

Colin Glass and Denis Jenkinson had brought their MkII Allard Dragon using 2-litre Bristol power, while two beautifully engineered dragsters were Harold Bull's 800cc BMC-powered Stripduster and Les Turner's blown 1500cc Ford slingshot.

The Dos Palmos blown Chevy Gas dragster, last seen at the Drag Festivals, was freshly imported from California by Bruce and John Ropner, Peter Godlee, Norman Barclay, and Gerry Belton; known as the Croft Drag Racing Partnership.

The last weekend in September at Blackbushe marked the start of the 2nd British International Drag Festival. This time eight AA/Fuel Dragsters and five drag bikes came over from America. Coupled to the growing field of British machines it promised to be a fantastic weekend, until the untimely arrival of drag racing's most feared enemy ... rain. The strip was wet all weekend but eliminations were run through the puddles. Even the American dragsters made some solo runs in the slippery conditions, which were mainly gentle squirts of power off the line, but the fans could hear the sound of blown and injected nitro power and knew that if the sun came out they would see some magic.

Geoff Jago, one of the UK's pioneer hot rodders, drove up in his straight-six Zephyr-powered Model T hot rod. Apart from the dragsters, all classes were for saloons, sports, and racing cars. Cars like Geoff's would later be classed as 'Altereds' but for now they were just causing havoc for the RAC scrutineer, who ended up failing it as it lacked a battery clamp, and he didn't like the suspension setup either. Things got worse when Mark Stratton and Dave Riswick turned up with the Anglo-American Anglia, a sit-up-and-beg Ford fitted with Jaguar power, but without front brakes it too failed scrutineering. Paul Hicks' wild Oldsmobile V8-powered Austin Cabriolet somehow got classed as a saloon. Unfortunately, carb problems kept him in the 18s, but for the fans it was still the wildest and fastest prewar Austin they had ever seen. Running in the same saloon class was John Bennett's wife, Ann, who clocked some mid 15s in their lightened and hopped up 1958 Pontiac.

Brian Witty was back out with an ohv Mercury-powered slingshot Nor'westerner that ran 16.16s at 92mph, while Allan Herridge got the DD Cadillac down to 12.38s.

John Harrison and Jeff Theobald had fitted blowers to their dragsters, and John had now replaced the old Atlantic motor with an Austin-Healey lump. Paul Manders' dragster had a 331in^3 Chrysler and a pair of

Jeff Theobold's wild-looking, Jaguar-powered dragster debuted at the first meeting of 1965 with four rear wheels, in an attempt to enhance traction. Later in the year, Jeff built a new dragster with just two rear wheels. (Courtesy Brian Sparrow)

transverse Wade blowers atop the hemi. Although it had a broken half shaft he brought it along anyway, and after checking out the American rails Paul decided to sell it and build a more modern design.

Alan Allard was out in the new Allard Chrysler dragster, featuring a longer stainless steel chassis with the Potvin blown hemi from the old car, and clocked some brave ten-second runs at 150mph.

The sun came out as the event ended, leaving everyone hoping for dry weather at a one day meet to be held at Woodvale a week later.

A reported 30,000 fans arrived at Woodvale,

Richard Wright's Model T used Cadillac power to make 14-second passes in Dragster Eliminator (there wasn't an Altered class yet in 1965). (Courtesy Brian Sparrow)

British dragsters were now being built for show as well as go, with Dragster Developments' Cadillac slingshot looking good alongside the American Dos Palmos. (Courtesy Brian Sparrow)

looking for nitro action and blue sky. They were not disappointed as the sun came out and Danny Ongais blasted into the seven-second zone with 7.99s in Mangler, and then it was time to go racing.

First out was Chuck Griffith wheelstanding his way to an 8.44s win over Nick Colbert's 9.05s. Danny Ongais then blasted his way into the history books again with the first 200mph pass at a quicker 7.91s to shut down Bob Keith. Next, Buddy Cortines upped the ante with a 200mph pass in a blistering 7.83s to literally blow away Tony Nancy. Finally, Gary Casady's 400 Jr, the only Chevy in a field of Mopar hemis, beat Ben Griffin. But his luck ran out when he met Cortines' Troublemaker in the next round, his 8.57s at 172mph out classed by Cortines' 7.86s at 192mph. Ongais blew his clutch with another 7.90s at 200mph, taking out Griffith's Starlight car that was close behind with an 8.11s at 198mph.

A frantic wrenching session to get a new clutch fitted saw Ongais' Mangler move to out-face Cortines for

John Harrison in the near lane prepares to take on Jeff Theobald through the Blackbushe puddles! (Courtesy Guy Griffiths)

DRAG RACING

NOV. 1965

2s 6d

The first magazine on the sport in Europe

IN THIS ISSUE

★ The Complete Story of the 1965 Drag Festival – PART ONE

★ Association News

★ Dragster Drivers form a Union!

★ Harold Bull's Dragster 'Strip Duster'

TOP AMERICAN FUEL DRAGSTERS RUN AT BLACKBUSHE DESPITE RAIN!

the finals in near dark. With nitro fire dancing across the headers, British fans had a true taste of AA/Fuel racing at its best. Sadly, it was a one horse race: the Mangler exploded its blower on the line as Buddy Cortines responded to the flag start, hitting on all eight cylinders and shaking the very ground as he thundered down the track, thrilling fans with their quickest, fastest, and most spectacular run yet, 7.74s at 201mph!

The British drivers were also making great strides with 9.30s and 168mph from Allard, the first nine by a British-built machine, while Norman Barclay went 9.72s and 163mph in the imported Dos Palmos.

Although there was some excitement when American bikes raced British bikes, "shambolic organization" meant there were no winners! The best numbers came from British rider Alf Hagon, whose blown JAP carried him to 147mph in 10.50s.

But no matter what, fans went home in awe of the stunning action they had seen from the awesome nitro-powered AA/Fuel Dragsters and their ground shaking seven-second 200mph races. Sadly, those memories would have to last a long, long time ...

Once again, the American dragsters received huge coverage in both British and American magazines. Drag Racing was later taken over by John Bennett and renamed Drag Racing & Hot Rod.

Santa Pod opens 1966

Things looked bleak for British drag racing after the International Drag Festivals. A planned BHRA drag race at Duxford had been cancelled due to noise complaints, and rumours were spreading that the track at Graveley was to be broken up for hardcore. It needed a permanent drag strip if the sport was to survive, so it was welcome news when at the BHRA AGM in October, chairman John Bennett announced that a new company, National Dragways, had obtained land around one of the main runways at Podington Airfield, Bedfordshire, an ex USAF B15 bomber base, with just that in mind. Previously used as a sprint location, it would be developed as Santa Pod Raceway in honour of Santa Ana dragstrip and the local village of Podington.

The five directors of National Dragways were John Bennett and his business partner Ted Peddle, Bob and Roy Phelps, and airfield owner Ernie Braddick.

By early 1966 Santa Pod was already booked up from April to October. Thousands of feet of fencing and wooden box crash barriers filled with stones were under construction, together with an impressive three-storey control tower situated in the centre of the strip behind the start line. Ind Coope, the famous brewer, was providing two kiosks, serving every imaginable type of refreshment including, of course, Double Diamond, and toilets were constructed. Another fixture was Jack Stillwell's 'Stripside Stores' selling T-shirts, hats, decals, and all the drag racing goodies a fan could want. Most importantly, Peter Billinton was designing and building the complex timing system and Christmas tree start

KOOL KAMS

The Official Newspaper of the British Hot Rod Association

NOVEMBER, 1965

ENGLAND TO HAVE FIRST PERMANENT DRAG STRIP

As announced at the AGM, a company known as National Dragways has been formed under the direction of our Chairman, John Bennett. This company will be developing a 90-acre site in Bedfordshire, and plans to construct a drag strip, complete with all facilities. The strip will be known as "Santa Pod Raceway", and the first events are scheduled for April 1966. It should be stressed that although the people responsible for this venture are all BHRA members, the strip will be operated entirely as a private commercial proposition.

Consequently, although BHRA will undoubtedly reap benefits from publicity, it should be understood that they are in no way connected with National Dragways financially.

J/T [illegible]'s 1962 T120 ss. (See "Winding On", P. 2)

MODEL DRAG DATES:

November 20th: National Model Drag Championship Finals at the new Elephant-and-Castle Shopping Centre main hall, London. December 19th, Grand Xmas Drag Meeting with appropriate prizes. To be held at Philips Croydon Works, Commerce Way, off Purley Way, Croydon, Surrey. Starts at 10.30 a.m.

EDITOR'S NOTES

COMPETITION

Here we go again with a new year, a new committee, and a new Kool Kams. By a unanimous vote at the AGM, Kool Kams will, in future, be published as a newspaper every month; there will be no more magazines. To mark this change-over, we have decided to give a fresh appearance to the paper starting with a new Title Heading. Over to you artists then; here's what we want! You can see from the Heading at the top of this page what area you have to play with. Design us a complete Heading to incorporate the title, "Kool Kams", and the words, "The official paper of the British Hot Rod Association", together with the month of issue. Remember that this is a hot rod association, not a drag racing organisation; therefore, try and steer clear of designs depicting dragsters. Entries can be in pencil or ink; it is the design we are looking for initially, so don't worry if your artistic talents aren't exactly brilliant. The winning design will, if necessary be reproduced by a professional artist.

To encourage entries in this contest, we will be awarding prizes as follows:- 1st, a chrome BHRA car badge; 2nd, a pair of BHRA cuff-links, and 3rd, a BHRA tie-clip. Naturally, we can only use one design, and the entries will be judged on the following points:- Impact, Simplicity and Appropriateness. With your entry, state briefly what you would like to see featured in Kool Kams, although this in itself will have no bearing on the result of the competition. The Editor's decision is final, and no correspondence can be entered into regarding the results. All entries must be received by December 15th, and should be sent to the Editor. Note that the contest is open to BHRA members only!

MEMBERSHIP . . .

continues to rise and is now in excess of 260. When you consider that we reached a figure of 323 when most members became due for renewal at August 1st, this is indeed encouraging. Of the 252 who were due for renewal, about half have paid their subscriptions, but there are still another 125 who haven't yet bothered. If you know of any such "defaulters", perhaps a well-timed boot applied to their posteriors would do the trick?

PETE BARTLETT.

Chairman's Comments

A NEW COMMITTEE year has begun; those of us who have been re-elected are pleased that members have shown their appreciation of our efforts in this way. There have been moments during the past year that many of us have been on the verge of crying "ENOUGH", but each time some new and challenging aspect of Hot Rodding has come along to make us press on still harder for the success of our Association.

The full size drag racing season has ended, for BHRA members it has been a very successful year, particularly in the dragster classes. It was unfortunate that the biggest event of the year, the Festival, should be so poorly handled, although the pre-event organising with its far greater difficulties was successfully carried through.

My sympathies are with Sydney Allard, the man who so obviously wants drag racing to succeed, and I can only hope that the results this year will not deter him from trying once again to popularise this exciting sport. I feel sure that our members would much rather see a selection of drag vehicles similar to the first year than eight near identical rails. Nevertheless, these eight were certainly top class machines although not all quite the 200 mph rails we were expecting. Whatever happened to Kallita and Schubeck?

BHRA's brightest year is ahead; forward planning by your Committee has put us in the enviable position of promoting in November this year the first British National Model Drag Racing Championship, and in August next year the full size Championship. Coupled of course with having the first permanent drag strip in the country, we can now expect our membership to grow even more rapidly.

All we ask of our members now is to join in whichever aspects of Hot Rodding they enjoy (tell us if there is one we don't handle), and watch those they are not so interested in.

Spend the dark nights browsing through your own personal magazine, Kool Kams, and have a thoroughly enjoyable hot rodding year. Don't forget also to tell your friends all about BHRA.

JOHN BENNETT

BRITISH HOT ROD ASSN.:

Annual General Meeting 1965

MINUTES OF the Annual General Meeting of the Association, held at Hednesford Hills Raceway, near Cannock, Staffordshire, on Sunday, October 24th, 1965. The Meeting commenced at 1.15 p.m.

Present were: Chairman—J. C. Bennett, Secretary—Mrs A. Bennett, P.R.O.—V. Oaten, Motor Cycle Secretary—R. Wayne, Midland Division Secretary—D. Withers, and Northern Division Secretary—C. Lingard.

Approximately 90 members were also present—nine from the Northern Division, fourteen from the Midland Division, four from the Southern Division, and the remainder from the Central Division.

The Chairman opened the meeting with a few words of welcome to the members, and conveyed the apologies of Committee members unable to attend. He then introduced the Committee members present.

The Treasurer's Report followed, read by the Chairman in the Treasurer's absence. The balance in hand was reported as £246-13-0d, a certified copy of the balance sheet was produced and a detailed description given of its contents. The Treasurer announced in his report that the forthcoming year's balance sheet would be in greater detail as a result of his proposals to re-organise the methods and entries in the Association's ledgers. The Association now has 250 fully paid members.

A. Herridge proposed that the report be accepted, this was seconded by P. Hicks and carried with a unanimous vote.

Statement of Accounts for Year Ending October 8th, 1965

Balance brought forward from 1964	90	14	7
General Income (Subscriptions, etc.)	469	12	6
	560	7	1
Less:			
Cost of various activities ...	65	13	7
Cost of administration ...	68	17	10
Cost of magazine and accessories	179	2	8
	313	14	1

Balance at 8th Oct. 1965: £246 13 0

Honorary Auditor: Mrs M. Bayer, 57 West End Court, West End Lane, Stoke Poges, Bucks.

As a result of the weather conditions the Chairman suggested that his report should be considerably shortened; the members agreed to this. The Chairman explained the general position regarding the current resignations and thanked those members resigning for their services, and those who had acted as temporary officers during the interim.

In the absence of the Editor, P. Bartlett, R. Wayne, the Motor Cycle Editor, read a report prepared by the Editor. The report explained the development of Kool Kams and Kool Kams Extra during the past year, and

(Continued on page 6)

Never had a headline looked so good! Welcome news indeed for Brits.

lights with a built in handicap system, while Captain Tom Hales was appointed as resident scrutineer.

The first drag race meeting at Santa Pod was held on Easter Monday by the BDRA and, after a week of sun, it poured with rain. A temporary roof was fitted to the unfinished control tower to keep the timekeepers dry, but a soggy Brian Holmes stayed out on the start line all day as chief starter for about 60 competitors who braved the elements. The first pass down the Santa Pod blacktop came from Harold Bull's Stripduster on a warm-up run. Class Eliminations were held for Production, Modified Production, Sports and GT, Racing Car and Dragster, followed by a Top Eliminator for the fastest eight cars at the end of the day.

Ken Bunce debuted Barons Barrow, a 2.4-litre Jaguar-powered slingshot that ran into the mid 15s.

Since the sport's inception in the UK, things were always happening in the north, and in March 1966 the BHRA's northern division, led by drag racing pioneer Clive Lingard, held Manchester's first High Performance Motor Show. As you can see, there was quite a diverse selection of vehicles on display. (Courtesy Mike Collins Archives)

D/D
2
GOODYEAR

Gerry Belton's Dragon, now called Dragonfly, was driven by Pete Atkins under the Watford Motor Accessories banner, while a young Chris Pattison had won the Works Dragon in a competition run by *British Drag Racing* magazine at the end of 1965 and he shared the driving with his dad. Ken Owen, Paul Hicks, and Clive Lingard built and supplied dragster frames and V8 speed equipment for other racers, and had entered Purple Heart, a 317in^3 Lincoln-powered slingshot. Sadly, the timing was out and the team spent most of its time putting out carb fires, and when it did get it running the Ford Pilot gearbox broke. Tony Densham took the Top Eliminator trophy running 12.32s at 122mph in the Worden to shut down Tommy McClone driving Les Turner's Ford dragster.

Sadly, just two days after the first meeting at Santa Pod, Sydney Allard passed away without seeing the fruits of his labours. It was a great loss to drag racing in Britain and his enthusiasm was sorely missed.

Whit Sunday saw the BHRA at Santa Pod for its 3rd annual Big Go and, thankfully, the sun came out. The timing equipment wouldn't work but this served to emphasise how drag racing differed from sprinting. Match races replaced timed runs with eliminations held

Six dragsters line up ready to go. From left-to-right: Hiding behind the marshal is Colin Glass in his and Denis Jenkinson's straight-six Bristol-powered device, Pete Atkins' Dragonfly, Harold Bull in Stripduster, then Tony Gane buried inside the red 500cc Rudge-powered Wicked Lady, with crew man Dennis Priddle standing tall alongside. Just in sight ahead of the VW is Derek Metcalf with Wombat, and finally, long-time sprinter Rex Heatley dwarfing his Grenfell Vincent. (Courtesy Ron Fisher)

in the afternoon. Wicked Lady, Tony Gane's 500cc four-valve Rudge-powered mini-dragster, had its motor hung out behind the rear axle for better weight distribution. Derek Metcalf's TR2-powered dragster now used an ohc Jaguar head. By lopping off two combustion chambers he had somehow grafted it onto his Triumph motor. The hemi-shaped Jag head and flat top Triumph pistons meant low compression, so Derek set about brazing half spheres of aluminium to the pistons; not one of his better ideas and when it fired up there were some interesting noises as the inevitable happened! John 'Hardluck' Harrison lived up to his new name after burning out clutches on a regular basis, doing it again at this meeting despite fitting a new racing clutch. He also blew a head gasket and melted a piston, so headed home to rename his car Jynx. Brian Witty was back out with a new chassis

Each meeting during 1966 saw more body panels removed from Mark Stratton's BSA Altered, but with the Chevy engine running sicker and sicker it kept him in the fifteens. (Courtesy Brian Sparrow)

on his dragster Nor'westerner, and Allan Herridge's Cadillac slingshot had been christened Pulsation.

For the first time there was a class for 'Altereds,' mixing street legal and competition cars. Geoff Jago was racing his Zephyr-powered Model T, and Martin Hill had driven up in his Oldsmobile-powered Model A Ford sedan. Mark Stratton and the Anglo-American Team had built a 265in^3 Chevy-powered 1934 BSA Scout, called Scout Master, and John Wright was there with his Austin pickup-bodied Jaguar-powered Altered. Bob Venison and Brian Gibson brought along their metallic purple Ford Popular called Wild Thing – fitted with the engine, 'box, and rear axle from a MkVII Jaguar. Colin Kettley was there with his Jaguar-powered Ratcatcher that featured a homemade body, and yet another Jaguar-powered Altered came in the form of Colin Dunster's Model Y Ford, called Juggernaut. Alan Allard had left the big dragster at home and brought along the company's latest strip blazer, the Dragoon Anglia. The 105E Anglia ran bonnetless with a Shorrock blown 1500cc Ford protruding from the hole. The front end was jacked-up 'Gasser'-style, and it had been painted Silver Metalflake by Geoff Jago.

The US Masters Commando Drag Racing Team came to Santa Pod for two weekends in June, organised by the BHRA and promoted by Bob George, with famed Super Stock racer and lawyer Al Eckstrand as captain. Bud Barnes and Bob Gladstone brought their AA/Fuel

Early British drag racing at its best! Juggernaut, with its back-seat driver, skinny, smoking tyres, and twisted body was a fan favourite. (Courtesy Mike Collins Archives)

Check out the tax disc and wipers. Seeing John Wright's Jag-powered beast on the street in the sixties must have scared little old ladies, to say the least! (Courtesy Ken Robbins)

Dragster Ultrasonic, while Gil and Dave Mudrak came over with The Runt, a blown Chrysler hemi-powered slingshot fitted with a 1923 Model T roadster body. For Funny Car fans, it was said that Dick Smith's 140mph Altered wheelbase Dodge Dart was coming, but it failed to arrive and they had to settle for Al Eckstrand's Dodge Charger stocker. An Anglia Gasser was on the team run by Larry Arnold, powered by an injected 327in^3 Chevy, while EJ Potter brought over his bike, also powered by an injected 327in^3 Chevy – no wonder he was called the 'Michigan Madman!'

The first weekend kicked off with Bob George introducing the Commandos to the spectators before they ran solo runs. Larry Arnold was getting very out of shape in the ten-second Anglia Gasser, as was Gil Mudrack in the Runt, who had three wheels off the ground in a wild wheelstand before adding some much needed weight to the front axle. Bud Barnes got an oil

Martin Hill's heavy street-driven, Old's-powered Model A against the super light Bristol dragster of Colin Glass and Denis Jenkinson. (Courtesy Ken Robbins)

Allan Herridge's years of sweat, strain and toil paid off when the Cadillac-powered Pulsation got into the tens early in 1966. (Courtesy Colin Underhill)

covering on one of his runs and, unable to see, wiped out the top end lights on Saturday. His best elapsed time (ET) over the weekend was 8.57s for a new strip record. The quickest British dragster at the meet was Pulsation, which Allan Herridge got into the tens with 10.84s. Long-time sprinter Rex Heatley, who carried his 998cc Vincent drag kart inside his estate car, sped to 11.96s along with Pete Atkins who ran 11.70s in his Dragon.

One week later, the US team were at it again. The Runt and Ultrasonic were run together. Gil Mudrak ran his best time at 9.03s, while Al Eckstrand clocked a best of 12.96s. EJ Potter got down to 10.48s at 142mph before crashing on his last run when the bike veered left and hit the barrier, ricocheting back across the strip and into the air, necessitating a short stay for EJ in Bedford Hospital. John Bennett was pleased to see his barriers stood up well to the altercation! Top Eliminator went to the incredibly quick Shelby Cobra of Gerry Tyack

Fitting roadster or coupé bodies to slingshot dragsters and then running them blown on nitro was popular in the USA at the time. The Mudrak brothers brought over this Model T roadster-bodied dragster with the US team. (Courtesy Brian Sparrow)

The control tower timekeepers get the thumbs up from Chief Starter Brian Holmes. (Courtesy Mike Collins Archives)

Gerry Tyack and Al Eckstrand provided some close, nail-biting racing, with both cars in the high 12s. (Courtesy Ron Fisher)

that ran a best of 12.86s and also blew Al Eckstrand's Charger into the weeds more than once.

The BDRA were back at Santa Pod on June 26th using a new Christmas tree start system with lights at the top of the tree indicating the position of the car in relation to the start line. With both cars lined up 'in stage,' a countdown of two amber lights led to the green. If a driver went too early they would get a red light and be eliminated. Many racers red lit before getting used to this, but Mark Stratton had a unique idea. On the first amber he would sing 'Eeny, Meeny, Miny, Go,' dropping the clutch on 'Go,' and it worked! A new dragster was Alan Blount's 241in^3 Red Ram Dodge hemi-powered slingshot, Weekend Warrior. Jack Fisher brought out Sod Buster, which was front-wheel drive with a 1132cc Mini Cooper motor. Brian Parkins arrived with a drag kart using a Keele chassis and 498cc Triumph motor, and Gerry Cookson was in Minor Leaguer, a neat little

Could you imagine straddling a few hundred horsepower of injected Chevy V8 and smoking the quarter-mile? They didn't call him the Michigan Madman for nothing! (Courtesy Ron Fisher)

Gerry Cookson's first of many drag racing machines appeared in 1966. (Courtesy Brian Sparrow)

slingshot using 950cc BMC power. Les Turner had added some nitro to the tank of his blown 1500cc Ford slingshot and recorded 10.843s, followed by an even quicker 10.840s at 117mph – a fantastic achievement for such a small engined dragster! Allan Herridge improved his time to 10.68s at 132mph, and Ken Cooper got his flathead into the 12s with 12.90s.

The first drag race for bikes at Santa Pod was organised on the 17th July by the BDRA. Alf Hagon set the top time of the meet. Smoking the slick for the first 200yds, he clocked 10.27s on his blown 1200cc JAP ... who needs Chevy power! Alf took the Big Bike Eliminator, beating Neville Borham. Next class down saw George Brown on top form with Super Nero beating Boris Ashwell with 10.48s. The 350cc Class saw Eamon Hurley take the win with 12.71s.

A few dragsters and Altereds were invited to the bike meet, including Nobby Hill's new Houndog III that had a stainless steel chassis wearing full bodywork. Using Cadillac power with a front-mounted Wade blower and homemade injection, driver Mike Hutcherson ran 15.57s.

The BHRA held its next meet on July 31st, which attracted the biggest entry so far seen at Santa Pod. An unscheduled glider landing on the strip during the day was a bit of a surprise to all, but everybody enjoyed beat group the Mosaics, which performed during the lunch break in front of the control tower, particularly its latest hit *Let's go Drag Racing*. Rex Sluggett towed up from the west country with his Duke of Cornwall blown Dodge hemi slingshot, not seen since Woodvale where it refused to fire. This time it fired but blew up before making the start line. He was to have faced the new Houndog III that Mike Hutcherson brought to the line, though he too was having troubles and lost fire so elected to push it through the quarter-mile to take the win, and with much urging from commentator Roger Wayne, recorded a seven minute run! Harold Bull was now using injection on his 950cc BMC, and had also added 20in to the wheelbase to aid stability. It worked

Pit marshal Bob Farrar checks off Rex Sluggett's Duke of Cornwall. Elimination boards stand ready at the back of the control booth – an old ambulance that did stellar duty. (Courtesy Brian Sparrow)

Mickey Thompson's Harvey Aluminum Special made a fleeting reappearance in the guise of the Golden Hind. It would later come back as Commuter. (Courtesy Brian Sutton)

He may be smiling, but RAC scrutineer Capt Tom Hales had refused to pass Liquidator without a firewall. (Courtesy Ron Fisher)

and he got into the 12s. Square One was back out, now fitted with an Oldsmobile V8, but never matched the 11-second ETs it ran when Riley-powered.

Alan Allard was getting quicker in the Dragoon Anglia, clocking 13.12s at the BDRA August 14th Trophy Meet. In fact, in one race he stalled off the line, managed to get in going again, and gave chase to his rapidly disappearing competitor, passing him just before the finish.

Some of the best drag racing so far seen in Britain happened at the BHRA National Drag Racing Championship over the August bank holiday weekend, and for the first time handicapping was used in eliminations.

Meeting by meeting the facilities were improving and there was now a shelter in front of the control tower for the start line crew. Wynns was very much in evidence

Wild Thing indeed, the Rat Fink team's Altered storms through the top end like a destroyer at the season-ending October meet. (Courtesy Mike Collins Archives)

Drag race! The Corvette's way ahead but that Jaguar is looking for a win, charging hard at the top end, despite the flooded track. (Courtesy Mike Collins Archives)

and its signboards now decorated the contol tower and barriers, as did its decals on most of the race cars.

A primrose yellow Ford Popular powered by a 3.4-litre Jaguar turned up, called Liquidator. It was unfinished, and Capt Tom Hales would not let Geof Barrett run without a firewall between engine and driver. Also out for the first time was the Golden Hind, built from what was still usable on the Harvey Aluminum Special left here after the 1963 tour. Tony Densham

Looking menacing with its roof chopped, the Liquidator thunders towards the finish line with its driver reluctant to lift off the gas too early. (Courtesy Mike Collins Archives)

had rebuilt it and taken it for some shakedown runs, but plans were already afoot to increase the wheelbase and for 'Fibre Glass Repairs' to make a full-length fibreglass body. After two days action, the 1966 Drag Racing Champion was Tony Gane with his tiny 500cc Rudge machine, and letters started pouring in complaining about handicapping!

The 1966 season ended as it had begun, with rain, but the BHRA still managed to run a successful meeting on October 2nd. Some of the faster cars did get a bit airborne as they aquaplaned through the puddles at the top end, including Rex Heatley on his Vincent kart that smashed into the top end lights. Thankfully, Rex and his kart escaped injury. This was Ken Cooper's meeting, as he not only won his class, but also took the Top Eliminator trophy against Harold Bull in the final, winning with a holeshot 13.89s to Stripduster's 13.43s. The Liquidator team had now fitted a firewall and was out racing, while another new Altered turned up in the hands of Alan Sherwin. It was based on a Ford Pilot chassis and running gear, fitted with a Ford Pop body, and called the Lurch. Alan Blount now had injection fitted to the Red Ram hemi in Weekend Warrior. The homemade system was built along the lines of a Hilborn setup, with eight ram stacks, a fuel pump made from a BMC Mini oil pump, and brake bleed nipples as injector nozzles. It ran smoothly in the pits, but gearbox troubles prevented any runs on the strip.

Alan Allard at last brought out the Allard Chrysler dragster, but not at Santa Pod. He entered it at Elvington for the annual records weekend and set a new two-way average standing start quarter-mile record at 9.336s. Also setting new records for their class were the dragsters of Les Turner, Harold Bull, and Tony Gane, and the Elvington records weekend became an annual trek for UK drag racers.

Raging racers mob John Bennett in search of recompense perhaps? No, just fun and games, with Harold Bull, Dick Lawrence, Don Beadle, Allan Herridge, and Ken Cooper. (Courtesy Mike Collins Archives)

Gathering speed 1967

As the 1967 season loomed, various rumours were circulating about large engine dragsters being built or changing hands. Cliff Jones was trying to buy the Dos Palmos dragster, while Phil Scragg was selling an unused Chassis Research dragster frame, complete with mag wheels and slicks, imported in 1963 by Motor Books and Accessories for Howard Parkin. Rex Sluggett had a 426in^3 Keith Black hemi complete with 6-71 blower and Crower injection ready for a new dragster, while Tony Densham's full bodied 427in^3 Ford-powered dragster was taking shape at Fibre Glass Repairs. With all these potentially quick machines about it was no surprise that Jack Stillwell was stocking up on Irving Drag Chutes at his Stripside Stores.

At the other end of the scale, Mini specialists and engine tuners Neville Trickett and Geoff Thomas launched a new kit car, the Opus HRF. With a tube chassis and fibreglass roadster body costing £199, it was ideal for British enthusiasts to build their own version of an American street rod. Eventually more than 250 were sold, with more than a few ending up on the drag strip.

Sunday March 12th saw the first practice meet at Santa Pod for 1967. An amazing 81 cars and 64 bikes turned up, boding well for a busy season. There was a neat little Topolino Altered in the hands of Ian Garbutt

Derek Metcalf had lengthened Wombat's chassis but still lifted the front, much to the fans' delight. (Courtesy Brian Sutton)

Stu Bradbury added some colour to the start line and later took over as Chief Starter. (Courtesy Mike Collins Archives)

called High Fever, powered by a flathead Ford V8. Les Field had been inspired by EJ Potter and built a similar bike by fitting a Chevy V8 in an old BSA frame. Les was having a few problems with the timing and spluttered up the strip, causing great amusement when viewed from behind as flames seemed to shoot from the top of Les' helmet and clouds of smoke appeared from under his armpits!

Ken 'Flathead' Cooper debuted a new dragster in 1967. Triple carbs atop the flathead were fitted with cut down kitchen sink u-bends, ten times cheaper than what was available in the American Speed catalogues. (Courtesy Brian Sparrow)

The BHRA's first race of the season on Easter Monday saw an entry of 70 cars and 6000 fans, which caused crowd control problems during the day.

Tony Gane was driving a new supercharged 650cc BSA dragster, while Dennis Priddle handled the diminutive Wicked Lady that won the 1966 Championship. Mick Wheeler's new dragster, Scorpion, had an 875cc Hillman Imp engine hanging out behind the rear wheels, with Mick laying on his back in front of it! Stripduster now had Indigo Blue Metalflake paint, and Gerry Cookson's BMC dragster had the new name of Trouble Shooter. Les Turner's 1500cc Ford dragster wore a set of Goodyear Blue Streak slicks, and clocked the top time of the meet, 11.083s at 125mph.

The Altered class was now divided into Competition and Street, and on the competition side were some wild machines with new names. Mark Stratton had completely rebuilt his 283in^3 Chevy-powered BSA

Robin Bolch ran another flathead-powered machine, based on a Ford Pilot chassis and homemade roadster body. (Courtesy Brian Sparrow)

Altered, with its longer chassis wearing a cut down body and the name Hustler. Disturbance was the name given by Roy Dennard and Brian Sutton to their Jaguar-powered Ford Popular, while Stagecoach was the East Essex Drag Racing Team's Jaguar-powered Austin Ruby.

King of the hill in name and power departments had to be Keith Sales' Chevy-powered Megalomania, a much modified MGB body with an E-type-style nose built by Fibre Glass Repairs. Despite being rather overweight, Keith used the power of his 396in^3 Chevy motor to drive around the 0.65s handicap given to Mark Stratton's Hustler in the Competition Altered final. Megalomania

Looking like a stocker but running down dragsters, Ian Demain's Zodiac was a real sleeper with V8 Mustang power. (Courtesy Brian Sutton)

Ian Richardson hangs on to his awesome 2-litre Moonraker on another eleven-second run. (Courtesy Brian Sutton)

also ran some close match races against Jack Le Fort's Ferrari 250, both cars running 13-second ETs.

On the street side, the field ran the gamut from Ian Demain's Zodiac, a real sleeper using Mustang V8 power, to Mike Collins' Half a Min, a Mini van radically customised into a bob-tailed pickup.

This was Roger Wayne's final event as commentator, with Steve Stringer and Steve Perry taking over from the next meeting.

Alan Ing was now running the ex-works Allard Dragon, renamed Sh-Uno-Who. First time out at the BHRA's April meet it beat Dennis Priddle and Harold Bull to take Top Eliminator.

The Allard Dragons were still doing sterling strip duty in 1967 with Alan Ing now in charge of the ex-works machine. (Courtesy Mike Collins Archives)

Purple Passion stood loud and proud in Violet Metalflake paint and purple perspex windows with a classy matt black and mirror finish alloy panelled interior. Brian Sparrow in *Drag Racing & Hot Rod Magazine* described the car as "... faultless in every detail." Sadly, you need more than good looks to go drag racing and Purple Passion's first outing in April saw a fuel pump problem keep it in the 15-second zone, although next time out it took Super Eliminator. At its third meeting the Jackson and Cottingham team had the Jaguar-powered Ford Popular running mid 13s and 107mph.

The BHRA's 4th annual Big Go held over the Whitsun bank holiday weekend saw more new Altereds in a record entry of 86 cars. Ruben Johnson's Wildcat, a Jago T with a 331in^3 Fire Power hemi, was immaculately turned out in Lime Green Metalflake, metallic green steel wheels, black chassis, and even black leather buttoned upholstery! It didn't take long for an Opus HRF to turn up at the drag races, with a pair at this meeting. The Jones brothers' Opus One used a Shorrock blown 1500cc Ford motor, while Clive Skilton, who raced an E-type Jaguar earlier in the year, had his own version of the kit, which he called the Henry T, with 997cc Ford power.

Purple Passion's lightweight fibreglass doors, boot lid, and one-piece flip front end were all fabricated by Jerry Jackson and Dave Cottingham. (Courtesy Mike Collins Archives)

A classic early British drag race, with Bob Eyre's backseat ride Juggernaut getting a holeshot on Clive Skilton's Henry T. (Courtesy Mike Collins Archives)

Monday's eight car Top Eliminator saw some large-engined machines going down to Harold Bull's Stripduster and Alan Ing's Sh-Uno-Who. This produced an exciting final. It looked like Stripduster was going to take it on a bye run as Sh-Uno-Who was having problems firing up, but Harold sportingly cut his motor and waited. The Ford fired and both dragsters came up to the line. Harold's experience showed as he got a slight holeshot, staying ahead of the more powerful Dragon, but Alan caught up and passed him just before the finish, winning with a best yet 10.874s at 122mph.

Gerry Tyack gave fans a glimpse of a rare Porsche Carrera GT and also provided the sound of a very high rpm missed shift – painful to say the least!

Gerald Tyack brings his exotic 2-litre Porsche Carrera GT up to the line alongside Martin Kent's Facel Vega.
(Courtesy Brian Sutton)

Over from Ramstein, Germany, US Serviceman Sydnor 'Red' Harris enjoyed smoking his 1955 Chevy off the line to mid 15s, and talked of plans being made to bring a whole team over from the USAF base in September.

June saw the return of Bob George's US Masters Commando Drag Racing Team, led once again by the Ultrasonic AA/Fuel Dragster. Ron Jellineck and Dave McCaig brought a beautiful dragster featuring a pair of fuel-injected 401in^3 Buicks. Built by Tommy Ivo, it was finished in Candy Apple Red with a neat upholstered cockpit.

Sadly, that was about it when it came to horsepower, although lawman Al Eckstrand was driving

Ron Jellineck suits up in preparation for another smoky nine-second blast in his twin-engined Buick dragster. (Courtesy Mike Collins Archives)

a 427in^3 Corvette Stingray on American mags and slicks. There was also a pair of Mustangs and Barracudas that looked neat, but that was about it, they were stock.

The American cars made some demo runs at the BHRA's two-day bike meet, with Brian Holmes giving the two Mustangs a classic flag start, then there was some thunder as the twin-injected Buick dragster smoked its way to a storming nine-second, 170mph quarter-mile.

You know Bud Barnes was not on a thunder run, but the power of an AA/Fuel Dragster on a wet track must have given an interesting ride! (Courtesy Brian Sutton)

Alf Hagon got his JAP down to 10.117s but kept pulling red lights, while Top Eliminator went to Pete Allen on his twin Triumph. A bonus was the running of Santa Pod's first night meeting on Saturday, with 14 cars invited for some match racing, pairings being set by drawing names from a hat. Racing started at 7.30pm, with several hundred spectators letting out a resounding "Ooh" when the track lights were turned on at 10pm. Derek Metcalf scored a first by becoming the first ever competitor to race under artificial light at a British drag race. Following some demo runs from the bikes under the lights, the American dragsters made a couple of late evening blasts to wrap up a spectacular evening.

A tremendous entry of 91 cars turned up the following weekend, and managed to get through most of their class eliminations before rain messed things up. Bud Barnes also set a new strip record, smoking Ultrasonic through the whole quarter-mile in 8.47s at 189mph. The neophyte fans went wild, but some who had witnessed seven-second, 200mph side-by-side races in 1965 felt a little short changed.

Those who had been mumbling about the lack of large capacity British dragsters all year were rewarded by the sight of the 427in^3 Ford-powered AA/Fuel Dragster Commuter. The beautiful full-length body was dripping in Red and Gold Metalflake, and everything else was chromed. Driver was drag racing pioneer Tony Densham, with Peter Billinton and Roy Phelps wrenching. Although the rain prevented any runs, the American mechanics helped the team set the motor up.

Alan Blount was back out with Weekend Warrior. Having blown up the hemi, it now sported a 283in^3 Chevy fitted with the team's homemade injection.

Things were looking good in the Competition Altered department. George Gillett's 1939 Austin Ruby had a jacked-up front end, and a huge Wade blower fitted to the front of a Jaguar engine; sitting way back in the driver's compartment it looked really wild. Its classic 'Gasser' look was aided by a Moon fuel tank and a pair of American mags on the rear with 'George is Draggin' painted on each door. A pair of new Ford Populars joined the fray; Pete Smith and Ed Gurney's Hushabye, this time Buick V8-powered on a 1938 Hillman chassis, and the Church brother's 289in^3 Ford-powered Gold Rush. John Wright's Kool Kams Austin pickup now had the cab moved back over the rear wheels, and Bill McGrath was driving Gloink, a Jaguar-powered 1956 Triumph roadster.

Set-back engines and back-seat drivers got the weight over the rear wheels for maximum traction. (Courtesy Mike Collins Archives)

The Chevy-powered Hustler in the far lane smokes out the hole alongside Gold Rush, which twists its way up the strip, thanks to

The Austin Ruby-bodied Stagecoach hazes the tyres ahead of Bill McGrath in his Triumph roadster Gloink: both were Jaguar-powered. (Courtesy Ken Robbins)

In Street Altered was the Van from Uncle, a bright orange Ford 300E van with a big Pontiac V8 shoe-horned in pushing Ken Stevens deep inside the back, sitting snugly under a roll bar.

RAC officials showed they were more than just a bunch of old fogies when, at short notice, they allowed an extra International meeting to be held on the first weekend of July after the rain had spoilt the last race, and the American team stayed over.

Commuter was back out and big Bob Gladstone squeezed himself into the tight cockpit for a push-start. As soon as oil pressure was showing Bob dropped the clutch and it fired first time. This put a smile on the team's faces, but when Tony Densham brought the car out for a run the following day the magneto drive broke. They were learning that getting an AA/Fuel Dragster to run, let alone perform, was far from easy.

Cliff Jones's Opus One now sported a 2500cc Daimler hemi, and Harold Bull had added a supercharger to Stripduster. Once again, the US Team did its stuff, including a hairy lane swapping run by Bud Barnes in Ultrasonic. Thankfully, it was a solo pass!

July 23rd saw the first running of the *Drag Racing & Hot Rod Magazine* Trophy Meeting. The Oldsmobile-powered Square One was back out after a long absence, taking out Stripduster with 12.742s at 100mph, but then losing to Ken 'Flathead' Cooper's 12.007s at 113mph. Alan Ing beat them all, taking Top Eliminator again and the DR&HRM Trophy.

The year had been a financial struggle for the BDRA, and it was wound up in August. The BHRA took on existing members and then, at the AGM later in the year, changed its name to the British Drag Racing & Hot Rod Association.

The first British Motorcycle Drag Racing Championship was held at Santa Pod on August 20th, and Alf Hagon was the star of the show. Fresh from his first nine-second run at Duxford, Alf gave fans the quickest two-wheel passes on the planet, a 9.935s followed by a fantastic 9.679s at 143mph. Alf not only took home the championship trophy and a new world record, he also pocketed some cash from John Bennet, who had promised to hand out £10 to anyone making a single-digit pass.

One week later, the cars lined up for the BHRA's 2nd Drag Racing Championship. The sun shone strongly, fans were walking around in shorts, and Mrs Taylor's tea bar was busy serving egg and bacon breakfasts to

After having a blower and injection fitted, Harold Bull's meticulously built Stripduster really began to fly. (Courtesy Mike Collins Archives)

Harold Bull and Derek Metcalf were now trading as B&M Equipment, supplying anything from small brackets to complete dragsters. (Courtesy Mike Collins Archives)

The 1967 British Drag Racing Championship held over the August bank holiday was blessed with Californian sunshine. Fans made use of whatever they could find to get a good view as Megalomania and Phaeton come to the line. (Courtesy Brian Sutton)

complete the scene. Practice runs commenced at 11am followed by racing up to 7pm on both days.

With Tony Densham fully suited-and-booted, the Commuter team came out intent on making a run. The FGR Plymouth pickup pushed the swoopy red car up the track to get the oil pressure up and was then bump started on the way back to the start line. The big Ford sounded strong as it was manoeuvred round behind the tower and up to the line. Densham rapped the throttle, the lights ran, Commuter moved, then bogged down before the engine roared and Tony, with his foot on and off the loud pedal, took it through the quarter with a 10.3s first timing ticket. Later in the day Commuter was back out, with the whole team more confident as they fired up and brought the car up to the line. Again, it bogged slightly, but Densham kept his foot on it, thundering down track in 9.1s – the quickest yet by a British-built car. The car returned to a standing ovation

Bob Phelps helps engage Commuter's push bar with the FGR Plymouth pickup that had been push-starting dragsters since Mooneyes' visit in 1963. (Courtesy Ron Fisher)

and John Bennett got his wallet out again. Sadly, back in the pits the Ford's camshaft drive was found sheared, and that was it for the weekend.

Allan Herridge, along with Tony and Don Beadle, debuted Motorvation, the Pulsation chassis with an injected 301in^3 Chevy running direct drive. Sounded good, looked great, but they couldn't get it running right. New to the track was Phaeton, a Jaguar-powered mauve slingshot designed, built and driven by Tony Brown, assisted by Tony Russell, and backed by Jack Stillwell's Stripside Stores. Tony pleased the fans by deploying one of Jack's Irving 'chutes each time out.

Hemini was Colin Kettley's latest creation, a Mini pickup with a 392in^3 Chrysler hemi stuffed in the bed! Sadly, even when it was later kitted out with fuel-injection, the beast never matched its wild and wonderful looks. Ian Garbutt was back out with a new Topolino Altered called High Fever II. The Tangerine Metalflake body was mounted further back with the rear wheels in the doors and was Buick V8-powered.

With Christine taking the Ladies Eliminator, the Skilton family nearly took home another trophy when Clive's Henry T met Charles Dawson's Triumph Vitesse in the Street Eliminator final, but Charles just took it with a holeshot 17.451s to Clive's quicker but losing 17.358s – Clive was learning the hard way about reaction times.

Competition Eliminator went to Ian Demaine, whose V8 Zodiac just beat Brian Harvey's Lotus Cortina.

Christine Skilton in Clive's E-type won the first Ladies Eliminator to be run at Santa Pod, taking out Di Floyd in Geoff Jago's Model T, then took the trophy win over Rachel Harvey. (Courtesy Mike Collins Archives)

Then things got hotter and heavier as Hustler and Stagecoach came to the line for Super Eliminator. Dave Riswick was driving Hustler and he and Pete Mylrea left the line together in clouds of rubber smoke, the Chevy taking a 12.438s at 115mph win over the Jaguar's 13.203s at 104mph.

Ken Cooper and Alan Ing came up to the line for the Championship title. They left the line together but halfway up both engines faltered, a full weekends racing showing its strain. Alan took the win light and the trophy to cap a fantastic weekend's racing.

At the end of September seven American muscle cars were driven over from the USAF base in Ramstein, Germany. Mike Collins did not need to think too long when he was asked to meet them off the ferry and escort them to the Pod. They cautiously followed Mike in his Mini through the centre of London and up the M1. What a sight that must have been in 1967. Mike had his windows down so he could enjoy the burble of all those big V8s behind him, and all was well until they hit the first roundabout!

Sadly, politics raised its ugly head when the US

Even sitting in the pits, with those tall ram stack injectors, Megalomania looked super tough, but super heavy! (Courtesy Mike Collins Archives)

Ing had a fantastic season, taking most Top Eliminators and the 1967 Championship trophy. (Courtesy Mike Collins Archives)

Quick reactions took Al Boucher past this rare semi hemi Chevy to the final of the Ramstein Club Eliminator, in which he defeated Tip Franklyn's powerful GT500. (Courtesy Mike Collins Archives)

servicemen found out they had driven all the way from Ramstein yet had to race amongst themselves and, to make things worse, it was raining.

A new pair of Altereds turned up at the meet. Pete Atkins' Slo-Mo-Shun was a 289in^3 Ford-powered Jago T, and Derek Benbow and John Fullerton's Orange Crate, a 303in^3 Oldsmobile-powered Ford Popular. MAB was a new straight-six Zephyr motored dragster making its debut with Reg Sommers.

Jack Daly's Turbonique rocket-powered kart was on hand to entertain the fans. Unlike Alan Burgess' kart at the 1964 Drag Festival, this one had a longer wheelbase and Daly drove it lying on his back. Nobody knew quite what to expect when the kart came up to the line, but following an initial bang the tiny machine slowly gathered speed leaving everyone wiping their eyes from the pungent fumes.

Clive Skilton won two eliminators on the same day when he won Competition Eliminator in his Henry T and then Super Eliminator with his latest acquisition, a 1964 Corvette Stingray.

A month later, Mike Collins took a team comprising Allan Herridge and Harold Bull's dragsters and the bikes of Pete Allen and Ian Richardson to Ramstein. Mike Doherty's famed *Drag Racing Almanac* for 1968 hailed this as "Another milestone of progress ..."

The British machines delighted the power starved crowd with 11-second smoky runs, while the GIs and Germans ran their season ending finals. Mike Collins also had a chance at redemption following his loss to Clive Skilton at Santa Pod when behind the wheel of Tip Franklyn's Mustang GT500.

Tip had lined up his Mustang for the Top Stock final alongside a Chevy Chevelle. A two-tenths NHRA handicap gave him the win, but the Chevy owner protested. Tip, happy with a winning season, suggested

Dale Price's Oldsmobile 4-4-2 was the star car of the Ramstein visit. The wet surface meant it just couldn't match its previous twelve-second performance, but it looked and sounded tougher than most! (Courtesy Brian Sutton)

a heads-up race for the title and the challenge was readily accepted. Turning round, he threw Mike Collins the keys and said "you're driving Mike an' don't screw up this time." Talk about a dream come true. This time Mike made no mistake, leaving hard with a holeshot on the Chevy, and took the win with 13.90s. Later at the club house, Tip Franklin presented his NHRA Top Stock

Mike Collins puts Capt Tip Franklyn's GT500 Shelby up against Clive Skilton's injected Stingray for a match race at the end of the day. Mike lost this race, but did better a month later in Germany. (Courtesy Mike Collins Archives)

Those were the days; back-seat driving for Ian Garbutt's High Fever II, and shirt sleeves rolled up for Ruben Johnson's hemi-powered Wild Cat! (Courtesy Ken Robbins)

trophy to Mike, adding with a chuckle; "I won the title, but you won the race."

Back at Santa Pod, motor racing entrepreneur John Woolfe, interested in drag racing, entered his powerful Holman and Moody prepared 427in³ Ford-powered Shelby Cobra in the Super Eliminator at the final drag race of 1967 late in October. He must have felt good

After the August Championships both the Allard Chrysler and Commuter made some demonstration runs at Crystal Palace. (Courtesy Mike Collins Archives)

when his 12.909s at 107mph beat Stagecoach to put his Cobra in the finals to face Hustler. Then John Woolfe learned about the true nature of drag racing when Hustler driver Tex Blake strapped a great holeshot on the Cobra and stayed ahead for the win.

Woolfe was amazed that a homemade, small block Chevy-powered machine could beat his race-prepped Cobra, suggesting to the Hustler team that fitting his seven-litre engine into Hustler would make it even faster. Mark's response was simple; "That's a Ford, make it a Chevy and we'll talk."

The Cobra also had a match race with a two-second handicap for Clive Skilton's Stingray, which John Woolfe lost two out of three, but that, too is drag racing.

Shortly after, Alan Allard put the Allard Chrysler dragster up for sale and Clive Skilton soon became part owner of the car, with plans to drive it in 1968 as the Allard/Skilton dragster aided by John Hume, while Roy Phelps began an interesting project; the Wheelie Stingray, an exhibition machine designed to complete the quarter-mile on the rear wheels.

Elvington's records weekend was visited by Commuter, with the team hoping to eclipse Allard's 9.37s standing start quarter-mile record.

Making the required two runs within the hour, Tony Densham shattered the mark with a rapid 8.811s, backed up by a 9.08s pass, which gave Commuter a new FIA World Record of 8.915s.

What a great way for a racer to finish a first season with a new car!

Sprint cars were still coming out to drag race, and here Mike Andrews in his Cooper/Jap pulls a holeshot on Opus One. (Courtesy Ken Robbins)

Battle of the giants 1968

Following two years of operation, flaws in the layout of Santa Pod had become apparent, and 1968 saw some major changes.

The start line was moved back 300 yards, the pits relocated alongside the strip, and earth bankings built up that allowed spectators a good view of the racing. The old tower now stood close to the left-hand side of the track's new top end, and two new control towers wearing Coca Cola livery were built each side of the new start line.

Major construction work was handled by contractors, but during that long hard winter volunteers helped in refurbishing the track and its environs. Lights were installed, wire mesh fencing put up, and white lines were painted everywhere. Staging lanes were provided, with space aplenty for push-starts, but most importantly, the full quarter-mile track and run-off area was resurfaced. Also over the winter, National Dragways had become a limited company and was now known as Santa Pod Raceway Limited.

Easter Sunday saw the final licks of paint still being applied to the new metal crash barriers, as the pits began to fill with exciting new machinery and drivers keen to try out the 'seven-second surface' in front of 10,000 fans.

With a much advertised best-of-three match race between Clive Skilton's Allard/Skilton rail and Tony Densham's Commuter being the big draw, both cars were obviously the centre of attention, until a Land Rover pulled into the pits towing another homegrown AA/Fuel Dragster. Rex Sluggett and Dennis Priddle had arrived with Tudor Rose, 178 inches of Priddle-built chassis fitted with Rex Sluggett's supercharged Keith Black hemi.

First round of the match race and Commuter's engine died before it staged, leaving the Allard/Skilton dragster streaking down the track to a 9.13s at 163.4mph solo pass. Then his brakes locked up, cracking the chassis and putting him out of action for the rest of the meet. The match race was over before it began, but Clive Skilton was awarded the win!

Regardless, the meeting saw Tony Densham running the quickest ET at 9.052s, Skilton's 163mph was the fastest, and new shoe Rex Sluggett had run 9.409s at 161mph in Tudor Rose. With three AA/Fuel Dragsters in the nines at over 160mph, everyone wondered who would be the first into the eights at Santa Pod.

Mark Stratton and team were there with Hustler

Santa Pod advertised the match race between Densham and Skilton, unaware that another big AA/Fuel Dragster would turn up. (Courtesy Mike Collins Archives)

Colin Saunders looks a bit apprehensive as he prepares to make a run in Mark Stratton's latest beast. (Courtesy Brian Sutton)

II, a new dragster fitted with two 283in³ Chevys. The chassis was an Owen, Hicks and Lingard item, and the homemade front axle looked remarkably like a gatepost that used to stand outside the Stratton household! Colin Saunders was the driver, but after two runs the clutch burnt out. In fact, quite a few machines had similar problems on the new super-grippy surface. Ken Cooper lost his clutch after a 12.01s run, while John Harrison not only blew his clutch but broke transmission as well – his luck was not changing.

Another pair of OHL-chassied rails were Bob Chamber's blown Ford V8-powered Banshee and Walt Ithell's blown 283in³ Chevy-powered Poltergeist. After a troubled two years, Nobby Hills had completely redesigned the supercharger and injection on Houndog III and was rewarded when driver Mike Hutcherson got some power out of the Cadillac, running 11.389s at 121mph. Alan Blount's injected Chevy-powered Weekend Warrior had a new chassis, as did Harold Bull's Stripduster, which was now direct drive. Another

Easter gave Santa Pod its biggest ever crowd, seen here on its feet waiting for Banshee and Poltergeist to race. (Courtesy Ken Robbins)

BMC-powered dragster was John Whitmore's Obsession, while Bill Haynes' Konkerer, a neat little dragster built in his garden shed, used 997cc Ford power. Geronimo caught the eye, a beautifully built nitro-injected 324in^3 Oldsmobile-powered slingshot driven by Mike 'Tik' Tickner. On a smaller scale was Bob Pigrim's 600cc Norton-powered kart.

Opus One had stepped up to a 327in^3 Chevy and Muncie gearbox, while Alan Sherwin's new Altered Travel Agent used a 1959 Bond body and Jaguar power. Alan's flathead-powered Ford Pop went on for another couple of seasons in the hands of Vern Foale and Mike Lintern who renamed it Sidewinder.

Making a welcome return to drag racing was Gerry Belton in his 289in^3 AC Cobra, while US airman Bill Satterly's ride was a Chevy II called Mean Machine; a real live American funny car, or at least a genuine Altered wheelbase A/FX machine campaigned in the States by Dick Harrell and Bill Thomas in 1965. Bill drove the 427in^3 Chevy-powered machine on several 12-second runs during the weekend.

Bill Satterly blasts out the hole in his Altered wheelbase Chevy II. Not many people realised Mike Collins was inside, wrapped around the roll cage, getting an in-car shot for *Drag Racing & Hot Rod*. All was well until the transmission exploded! (Courtesy Mike Collins Archives)

Tik Tickner gets ready for a run in the nitro-injected Oldsmobile Geronimo, the first unblown dragster in the nines outside the USA. (Courtesy Ron Fisher)

Pete Allen was on hand, making some smoky demo runs on his twin Triumph, before leaving with his bike for Australia.

One week later and the bikes took over at Santa Pod for their Season Opener. Alf Hagon seemed to like the new surface and laid down his quickest run yet; 9.644s at 148mph.

A man of action, John Woolfe had provided a fully loaded L88 427in^3 Chevy Rat motor for Hustler. The wild Altered was also sponsored by John Woolfe Racing, a company formed by Woolfe, Dave Riswick, and Arnold Burton to supply high performance parts. First time out at the May 5th meet the big block carried Mark Stratton to 13.05s at 102mph. Not having so much fun was John Harrison, who, with an Allard V8 gearbox fitted after his Easter blow-up, again cooked the clutch. Allan Herridge debuted the 1968 version of Motorvation, featuring a longer and lighter chassis, and simple bodywork made from paper-thin magnesium.

The 5th annual Big Go at Whitsun saw 17 nine-second runs as the big dragsters went hunting for an eight-second ticket. Top speed went to Tudor Rose at

The Watford Motor Accessories team ran two cars in 1968, Slo-Mo-Shun and Co-Mo-Shun. (Courtesy Ken Robbins)

179mph with a 9.097s ET, while Commuter suffered a broken blower belt. Les Turner kept Ford fans happy with a stunning 10.2s at 132mph from his blown 1500cc slingshot. Mark Stratton also stepped up, smoking Hustler to 129mph in 11.1s.

Clive Skilton marched through eliminations with runs below 9.20s at speeds above 160mph, setting the low elapsed time of the race with an oh-so-close 9.005s thanks to a well placed foot in the timing beams! The car's performance was a credit to John Hume, who set the car up, and the team who kept pace with Skilton's seemingly endless string of low nine-second power blasts.

The Top Eliminator final saw the Allard/Skilton rail staged alongside Taxi, Brian Ringsell's 354in^3 Chrysler hemi, in the wet! Skilton left behind a trail of smoke and spray, running 11.40s at 129mph to win.

Brian and Mick Gleadow's Ford Popular Altered Mangler had used flathead V8 power, but now ran an Oldsmobile, while Derek Metcalfe's new Stripstar dragster used a Wade blown 2-litre V4 Ford and was a rolling advert, using a chassis, mag wheels, and body panels all from B&M Equipment.

Saturday June 15th saw the first night meet of 1968. Roy Phelps brought out his Wheelie Stingray and had no trouble yanking the front wheels off the ground. The problems started when he tried to keep them up, but he was slowly learning the subtle art of driving a 'Wheelie' car.

It rained at the Summer Match Race Meet on July 7th, but Tik Tickner drove 'Geronimo' to 10.901s at 136mph, then tipped the can and ran 10.05s at 143mph – quite a statement from such a new team.

Houndog III also joined the ten-second club, with 10.9s at 105mph, as did Mark Stratton with Hustler's new slicks providing the traction for 10.71s at 134mph.

The Night Meet on 20th July had more than just magic in the air, it had the smell of nitro, with Geronimo coming up to the line with 33 per cent in the tank, and 9.973 seconds later becoming the first unblown dragster outside the USA to run a nine.

Commuter and Tudor Rose staged side-by-side for the first time, thrilling fans with the sound and the fury of two British-built AA/Fuel Dragsters barking in the crisp evening air. It proved too much for Rex Sluggett. Young and excited, ready to race for the first time, he red lit. Tudor Rose smoked hard off the line, with Densham charging hard behind to run 9.036s to Sluggett's 9.312s.

Forty minutes later, the big AA/Fuel Dragsters fired up again and the fans went wild, the air again heavy with the sweet smell of nitro as they staged. Again, an over-excited Sluggett red lit, but thundered to a top speed of 180mph as Commuter suffered a broken camshaft, bent valves, and popped pistons.

Clive Skilton's Allard/Skilton dragster was racing in eliminations and made it to the finals were he met Hustler. Mark Stratton tried hard with a holeshot 10.95s at 124mph, but Clive blasted past and took the win with 9.543s at 148mph.

The *Drag Racing & Hot Rod Magazine* Trophy Meet on August 4th was very wet, and Ken Obee's Lotus Seven aquaplaned out of control, hitting the top end barriers at speed, but he was unhurt. With no respite from the rain, the meeting was cancelled and a re-run held the following Sunday that saw history being made.

The Allard/Skilton and Tudor Rose dragsters could not make it as they were in Sweden for the Swedish Hot Rod Association's first Big Go, but Tony Densham, who had been away all week on business, arrived by plane in order to make the meet. Peter Billinton had set up Commuter to fly, and fly it did, blasting down the quarter-mile to 173mph in 8.891s! The fans went wild at the first British homegrown eight-second run at Santa Pod. Tony Densham got a rousing ovation as he was pushed back to the start where a smiling John Bennett handed over £50 for his historic effort. There was more to come, and forty-five minutes later Commuter came back out, storming through in a mind-bending 8.459s at 180mph! The quickest ever run from a British driver, and a new track record.

Elimination action had side-by-side nitro racing with Allan Herridge driving to a 10.279s win at 142mph over Tik Tickner's 10.703s at 144mph.

Then race fans got to see one of the great British drag races when Motovation faced Alan Blount's Weekend Warrior in the final, a pair of injected Chevies side-by-side. Herridge was loaded with nitro while Blount had petrol in his tank. Blount's holeshot left

Hey man, this was the sixties; hot rodders didn't wear fire suits! Freddie Whittle takes on the Austin Ruby of George Gillett. (Courtesy Mike Collins Archives)

Invader was the UK's first flip-top Altered and, with the body up, the attention to detail was apparent. (Courtesy Mike Collins Archives)

Herridge sleeping on the line. Motovation gave chase but his 10.462s at 141mph just could not catch Weekend Warrior's 10.712s at 123mph, which showed neophytes that in drag racing the fastest cars do not always win.

Three new Competition Altereds made the scene, led by Colin Mullan and Ruben Johnson's beautiful Invader, a steel one-piece Viva bodyshell painted Candy tangerine, hinged at the back it flipped up, looking every inch like a mini version of a Stateside funny car, complete with a 392in^3 Chrysler hemi.

Shutdown used a more traditional Model B Ford body beautifully hand formed by Freddie Whittle in aluminium, painted in Red Metalflake and using 265in^3 Chevy power. Good Vibrations was the name of John and Tony Dickson's new Ford Popular Altered powered by a 394in^3 Oldsmobile V8.

That same weekend in Sweden, Rex Sluggett was hobbling around on crutches having had his foot run over by the Allard/Skilton's rear slick while helping stage the car. This put Dennis Priddle in the hot seat, and he did a more than credible job. His first pass found him blasting off the line with Tudor Rose smoking the full quarter-mile to record a fantastic 8.53s elapsed time on a warm-up run! The Swedish fans went nuts. And even more so when the first race between the Allard/Skilton and Tudor Rose took place. Both cars lifted the front wheels, with Priddle getting things back under control to run 8.88s. The second race was again won by Priddle, while Skilton's chute failed to open, and the final saw Skilton making a banzai blast only to bang the blower, letting Priddle through to win three straight.

On the way home, Skilton decided it was time to rebuild the hemi with a top mounted blower for 1969.

The last of the season's night meets on Saturday August 17th saw Commuter and Tudor Rose back out together for the 'Battle of the Giants.' Word had got out that the Swedish timing system had been made by local

Tudor Rose thrilled Swedish fans with smoky eight-second power blasts, captured in this cover shot by Ake Wremp.

Densham and Priddle returned to the start line to a wild reception from the fans. The two AA/Fuel Dragsters looked superb under the lights. (Courtesy Mike Collins Archives)

Rex Sluggett's look of dejection suggests this shot might have been taken following a red light loss in Tudor Rose. (Courtesy Brian Sutton)

students so the times were treated rather loosely, and it was going to be interesting to see what the certified Santa Pod clocks had to say. Priddle was still in the hot seat and ran a couple of twitchy nines before Densham came out and ran an arrow-straight 8.68s at 176.6mph. The Tudor Rose team just stood in amazement.

Race time arrived and night had fallen when the call up lights blinked on. Commuter and Tudor Rose moved into stage with nitro fumes rising in the air. Two green lights and both machines launched hard with Priddle just in front, leaving the start area obliterated by a wall of tyre smoke thirty feet high. 8.87 seconds later the win light was glowing in Priddle's lane, Densham had lifted unable to see for smoke. Nobody doubted the Swedish times now.

Thousands of fans flocked to Santa Pod for the 1968 Drag Racing Championships held over the August bank holiday. Sunday was spoilt by rain but Monday was bright, and once again the two most powerful machines

The final AA/Fuel matchup at the August championships saw Densham red light, while Priddle blasted to top times of the meet with 8.46s at 171mph. (Courtesy Mike Collins Archives)

in Europe were barking nitro fire at each other as they moved into stage. Rex was back in Tudor Rose and the flames licking out the headers were an indication he had more nitro in the tank; the Keith Black hemi had never sounded so good. No one knew quite how much nitro was in the big Ford but Peter Billinton had a knowing smile on his face. The lights ran and yet again Sluggett dropped the clutch too soon, leaving a red light glowing as Densham stormed after him and still got there first with 8.52s at 167mph to 8.69s at 160mph from Sluggett. The fans went crazy at the first ever side-by-side eight-second race at Santa Pod, and one hour later Priddle was back in the hot seat with the crowd on its feet as the two cars moved into stage. Engine revs climbed, two greens, and away they went with Priddle getting a good two car-lengths holeshot, smoking the slicks for the full quarter-mile. Densham tried hard but could not reel in the charging Keith Black-powered Tudor Rose as Priddle took the win with his holeshot 8.88s at 148mph to Densham's quicker and faster 8.83s at 166mph.

Before the next race, the Sluggett/Priddle team dropped the pressure of its super sticky Goodyear slicks to 10psi in the hope of getting some extra ponies to the ground. Tudor Rose still smoked hard off the line, then the slicks dug in and it recorded the top times of the meet, an 8.46s at 171mph, while Densham had pulled a red light then got out of shape and wisely shut off.

Elimination action was just as exciting. Motovation's timing chain broke, but Mark Stratton came to the rescue, and Herridge and the Beadle brothers got the injected Chevy back together for the championship run against Geronimo. Tickner got the hole shot, but Bootsie ran him down to win the title with 9.907s at 141mph to 10.074s at 144mph. It was close.

Hustler won Super Eliminator with Mark Stratton beating Tony Brown's Jaguar-powered slingshot, while Competition Eliminator was dominated by two cars which met in the final, the Mercury Cyclone of Rod Alonso and Joe Copp's mighty Maverick 1957 Chevy. The Chevy fans cheered as Joe took the win with 13.64s to Rod's 14.86s.

The 1968 championships was Santa Pod's most action-packed drag race, but many racers wounded their steeds trying to get power to the ground. George

Pioneer drag racer Allan Herridge had tears in his eyes after winning the 1968 championship title with the first nine-second Junior Fuel pass outside the USA. (Courtesy Mike Collins Archives)

Gillett threw the big ends all over the strip from his Austin Ruby, while Ruben Johnson and Colin Mullan said goodbye to Invader's 392 hemi when it ventilated the block. Ian Garbutt was back out with High Fever II, now 352in^3 Ford-powered, and blew the gearbox after throwing a mean shift – but then no one ever said that drag racing was easy, or cheap!

The Elvington Records Weekend saw Tudor Rose make the long haul up from the West Country in search of a new standing start quarter-mile record, and it did it, thanks partly to helpful officials who let the team wait for a special delivery from Wynns after a warm-up run blew the oil filter. With just six pounds of air in the big Goodyears, Dennis blasted Tudor Rose to a smokeless 8.291s, backing it up with an 8.301s in the opposite direction within the hour to produce an 8.296s average for the new record.

1968 Motorcycle Champion John Hobbs was also in town, running 60 per cent nitro in the tank of his blown Triumph twin and breaking three World Records and four British records – not bad for a homegrown bike! Dave Lecoq's wild VW-powered bike was after Alf

Alf Hagon on his way to 157mph in a mind-blowing 9.3 seconds at the rained out Motorcycle Championships. (Courtesy Mike Collins Archives)

Hagon's 9.954s record. He shattered it with a one way mark of 9.859s, but on the back up run a main bearing gave up slowing him to 10.1s, close but not close enough. Weekend Warrior had been running under the record mark all year, but Alan Blount had problems on the day and went home empty handed, unlike the Hustler II crew, now running under the John Woolfe Racing banner that cracked its class quarter-mile record.

Once Tudor Rose had been torn down and certified legit by the FIA officials, Sluggett and Priddle loaded up the dragster and headed down to Santa Pod looking for some action at the Autumn Match Race. When they arrived, Commuter had already run 8.75s.

Rex donned his fire-suit and climbed into Tudor Rose for a warm-up run. He stormed off the line, getting out of shape, and taking out the timing lights and a front tyre, to clock 9.42s with a new track speed record at 182mph!

Allan Herridge loaned the Tudor Rose team his front wheels, and at 7pm a couple thousand fans still filled the banking waiting for the big race of the day. Dennis came out in Tudor Rose, followed by Commuter, as the air filled with nitro fumes. Tony gave his usual "two pints please" sign to the crew and both cars moved into stage. Two greens lights and Priddle got the holeshot again, leaving with Densham in hot pursuit. Tudor Rose got crossed up and lifted 100 feet from the traps, but still won at 167mph with a new track record of 8.28s.

Motovation had a one-second handicap and Allan Herridge had his best-ever run at 9.75s, which was just beaten by Commuter's 8.75s in this classic match race. (Courtesy Mike Collins Archives)

Commuter popped the blower, crossing the line belching flames with 8.77s at 157mph.

Following a mind blowing power display of drag racing machinery down Silverstone's pit straight organised by Mike Collins at the annual BRDC Gold Leaf Clubman's Championship in October, Players cigarettes engaged in talks with Mike about sponsoring a drag race series in 1969. When he relayed this to the powers that be at Santa Pod the response was an extremely blinkered and naive "no one's putting their name on this drag strip ..." Neither Mike nor the Players people could understand why. That same winter Colin Chapman's Formula One cars were dressed in the famed John Player Special livery. Can you imagine how British drag racing might have turned out had the invitation been accepted?

The year ended with a pair of new-style combined car and motorcycle race meetings, and for the first time drivers and riders had to qualify in order to race in Eliminations. Sadly, a lot of guys went home without racing. All classes now had Top and Junior Eliminators with the system good enough to be adapted for the 1969 season. They even allowed for any excess of competitors with a standby Middle Eliminator.

John Fullerton and Derek Benbow turned up at the end of the year with their new Altered powered by a 322in³ Buick. It had a Jago T body complete with turtle deck, so they called it Turtle T. Bruce Brown had bought the ex-Allan Herridge Pulsation chassis and fitted a 283in³ Chevy, calling it Prospector.

The final event, fittingly called the 'Last Chance,' saw Harold Bull make up for his season-long struggles with his new direct drive setup, by wheelstanding his way to a stunning 10.14s at 133mph to take Top Eliminator. It was December, and chilly, to say the least!

Thanks to Players Gold Leaf, circuit race fans received a taste of nitro power, the Silverstone stands filling when Commuter barked into life. (Courtesy Mike Collins Archives)

End of an era 1969

1969 got off to a fantastic start when 9500 people invaded Croydon's Fairfield Halls complex to enjoy the BDR & HRA's January show, featuring a colourful display of drag racing machinery and some amazing movies of stateside track action. Centre of attraction was the new Tudor Rose. Dennis Priddle had built a super-long 201in chassis utilising some new ideas, including one he had seen at the 1965 Drag Festivals on Danny Ongais's dragster: building it from two separate halves joined behind the engine, making it easier to access the clutch. The car had just been completed before the show and lacked final paint and chroming, but looked set to run straight through the sevens and into the sixes.

A new shop at Santa Pod now replaced Stripside Stores, located behind the startline on the right-hand side and run by Dick Lawrence, who called it 'Dicks Place.' The shop sold all the usual drag racing goodies, including colourful 'Roach' T-shirts from the USA. The control towers were now painted Castrol colours, and new commentator John Hall took over on the mike.

The Easter bank holiday weekend saw 10,000 fans turn up for the season opener and Santa Pod was blessed with fine weather, but where were the big AA/Fuel Dragsters? Clive Skilton was waiting for parts for his dragster, and the Sluggett/Priddle team had sadly split up. Rex was selling the Keith Black hemi while Dennis kept the chassis.

Santa Pod's ever faithful Commuter came out and clicked off an 8.848s at 141mph while burning rubber through the full quarter-mile, much to the fans' delight.

With no one to race, Tony Densham was matched up with Harold Bull in Stripduster, which was given a two-second start. Harold left the line with the front wheels in the air then headed for the centre line. From

1969 saw the Wheelie Stingray turning full quarters on the rear wheels (front wheels off the ground for the entire quarter-mile), and also making the cover of *Hot Car*, which described it as "the finest piece of customising that *Hot Car* has ever seen."

Sluggett and Priddle's super-long Tudor Rose II appeared at the BDR & HRA show in January. Then it vanished! (Courtesy Mike Collins Archives)

Dennis Priddle's new ride for 1969 was Whistler, a purpose-built Reliant Scimitar sponsored by John Woolfe Racing using Hustler's old 427in^3 Chevy for power. (Courtesy Mike Collins Archives)

then on it was 'hearts in the mouth' action as Commuter gave chase, not quite catching Harold who crossed the finish line first with 10.684s at 127mph to 9.266s at 152mph.

John Siggery was now driving Geronimo, and he took Top Dragster first time out, then beat Tony Anderson's new Ford V6 dragster Trouble and Ken Cooper's Bazooka Too.

John Whitmore had renamed his BMC dragster Climax and won Middle Dragster. Invader, now running Joe Copp's small block Chevy motor, lost the Top Competition title to Ed Gurney's Buick-powered Hush Too – a new name to go with his psychedelic painted AC body.

Top Bike went to Dennis Norman on his double Triumph.

At the May 4th Spring Match Race, Tony Densham took the ride of his life, driving Commuter on its quickest and fastest ever quarter-mile, thundering down track trailing a huge rooster tail of smoke to stop the clocks in 8.228s at 181mph – then his chute failed to open!

There were some diverse cars to enjoy. Walt Ithell's Aggravation dragster was now powered by a pair of 312in^3 Ford V8s. Nobby Hills turned up with Houndog IIII, which was again Cadillac V8-powered but with a top mounted supercharger and no longer full-bodied. Kevin Pilling debuted a 324in^3 Oldsmobile-powered Altered that was called Pure Seven as it used an Avon Special Austin 7 body, while Dave Collis was the new driver of Opus One.

Rain spoilt the five-year sunshine record at the annual Whitsun Big Go. It was to have been Europe's first three-day drag race but Saturday was wiped out by the wet stuff.

Kevin Burrows and team's Chevy-powered Malibu Express slingshot made its first appearance. It had a full-length body complete with cockpit canopy and was painted Blue Fire Flake. The team also brought a mobile workshop and soon had a thriving repair business as

Bill Haynes now had a new B&M chassis on his Ford-powered Quarterhorse slingshot, sparkling in the early morning Santa Pod sunshine. (Courtesy Ron Fisher)

The Chevy-powered Opus One ran strong and looked good, despite years of hectic track action, while Pure Seven waits to be unloaded. (Courtesy Ken Robbins)

other competitors made more use of the resources than they did!

Once again, John Siggery drove Geronimo to Top Dragster glory, a 10.397s taking out Ken Cooper's 11.068s. Apparently, Siggery had vowed not to touch a drop of his favourite whisky until he had run a nine, and he didn't have to wait long, winning his third straight title at the June Spring Nationals with 9.897s at 141mph.

Rick Fielding in his 1200cc Ford Competition Altered Imagination took the Junior Comp win.

Allan Herridge made his first appearance of the year at the Summer Spectacular in July with his renamed Glacier Bearing Special, showing the team had gained much needed sponsorship. Straight off the trailer, it ran 10.01s to head Top Dragster qualifying, only to go down to another title-winning charge from Geronimo in the final.

John Lloyd took Top Bike on his supercharged 998cc Vincent Romulus.

Fans had some close up excitement in the fire-up road when the push bar collapsed on Gerry Cookson's Trouble Shooter dragster just as the engine fired, sending it sideways into the guard rail and rolling. Gerry was uninjured but the dragster was badly damaged, leaving many racers taking a close look at their push bars, adding extra bracing where needed.

A team of racers went to Sweden in July, including Clive Skilton, who was back out with the Allard/Skilton dragster that looked good with a new white paint job and top mounted blower, but it couldn't run quicker than 15

Ziggy Smith waits patiently in his Daimler hemi-powered Anomalous, a wild-looking street legal Opus hot rod. (Courtesy Ron Fisher)

The Benbow & Fullerton team reappeared in 1969 with a rebuilt and lighter Buick-powered Turtle T. (Courtesy Ken Robbins)

seconds. Allan Herridge and the Beadles had a look and suggested a different fuel pump, loaned him one, and the car was back in the nines. Meanwhile, Commuter was running eights, until one of the very expensive aluminium rods punched a hole through the side of the big Ford. Sadly, this put it out of action for the rest of the year, so British fans had gained one AA/Fuel Dragster but lost another.

Roy Phelps and the Wheelie Stingray had the crowd on its feet when his continued patience and determination eventually produced a full quarter-mile run with the front wheels in the air at the August 3rd All Stars Meet.

Two weeks later and drag racing returned to Woodvale. The Top Competition final brought the crowd to its feet as the big 427in^3 Whistler faced the smaller Buick-powered Hush Too. Ed Gurney blasted out the hole ahead of Dennis Priddle, taking the win with an 11.67s to a quicker 11.56s. Clive Skilton was back out with the Allard/Skilton dragster, and the final of Top Dragster saw the big blown Chrysler up against John Siggery's injected Oldsmobile. Surely Geronimo couldn't take Top Dragster again? Stu Bradbury waved the flags and they left the line together. Clives hemi bogged slightly, giving Siggery just the chance he needed. Consistency tells in drag racing and Geronimo did it again with 9.789s to Clive's 10.105s. Back at the pits Clive discovered one of his plug leads had broken down and his dragster had been running on only seven cylinders.

The 4th annual Drag Racing Championships got under way over the August bank holiday weekend. Some fans turned up with their tents on the Friday,

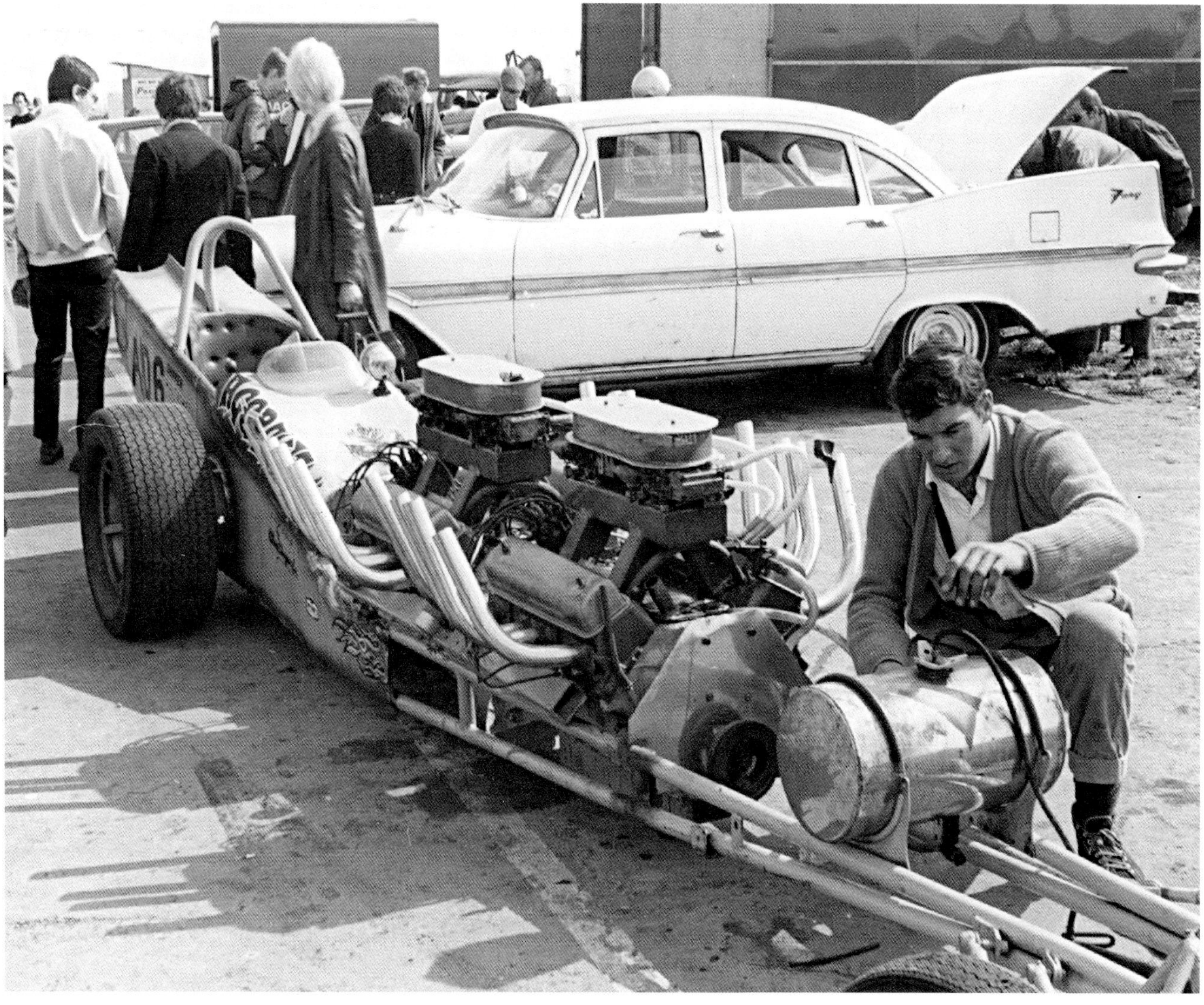

Walt Ithell's aptly named Aggravation gave him plenty of that in 1969, with two 312in^3 Ford V8s fitted. (Courtesy Brian Sparrow)

coming from all over the country as well as from Sweden, France, and Germany to see the 88 cars and 50 bikes do battle. John Whitmore now had a blower and injection set up on his BMC dragster that was begining to look almost identical to Stripduster. Brian Ringsell now had a Hilborn injected GMC blower atop the Hemi in Taxi, and still drove without face mask or gloves! The extra power contributed to a clutch explosion, with large chunks of flywheel reaching the spectator banking, fortunately, without finding a human target. A rule change followed.

New to Competition Altered was Dave Chester's Poacher with Jag power and a flip top Mini body, while new to the Street Altered ranks were Roland Pratt and Mike Derry with Kay-otic, a Chevy-powered Vauxhall PA Cresta. Russ Ward was out running his street-driven Jaguar-powered Ford Popular, and Peter Bennett was running a 289in³ Ford-powered Corsair while waiting delivery of a new injected Chevy dragster being built by Allan Herridge.

A new Cadillac motor in Houndog gave Mike Hutcherson a smoky 10.66s at 108mph, while John

Side-by-side blown and injected nitro-burning dragsters sounded good and looked great, as 'Snabba' Clive Skilton takes on 'Movin' Mike Hutcherson. In truth, their performance was sadly lacking when compared to the previous season. (Courtesy Mike Collins Archives)

Two years on and Invader's still a class act; its smooth lines and that gorgeous Candy Tangerine paint keeping fans happy, even when parked. (Courtesy Ken Robbins)

Siggery ran an easy-looking 9.95s in Geronimo and Clive Skilton qualified the Allard/Skilton for Top Dragster with 10.08s.

This time Skilton's dragster was firing on all eight cylinders as it came out to face Geronimo, again in the final. The injected Oldsmobile had been taking Top Dragster with consistent high nines all year, but this time the big blown hemi was too much. Clive took home the win and the Dragster Championship trophy with 9.66s at 156mph to Siggery's 9.87s at 129mph.

Mark Stratton did a fine job tuning Whistler and Dennis Priddle took the Competition Altered Championship crown with a strong a 10.587s at 129mph.

USAF Serviceman Doug Harler became Street Champion in his Dodge 440 Charger, while Mick Butler took the Bike Championship.

A meeting was run at RAF Hullavington in September and the Allard/Skilton rail made more crowd-pleasing smoky runs, but times stayed in the high nines, in fact Clive never managed to better his 1968 times. Brian Sparrow wrote in *Drag Racing & Hot Rod*, "L'Equipe Allard/Skilton suffered from too many chiefs and not enough Indians."

After years of trying to get his Austin-Healey dragster Jynx to run properly, John Harrison drove it into the mobile control tower, which really did become mobile, after getting out of shape trying to fire up. John took the mangled chassis home to use as foundations for a new, longer garage as his thoughts turned to building a twin-engined Austin-Healey dragster!

The season's final meeting at Santa Pod in October got off to a late start, when the doctor and ambulance failed to appear on time, and it ended in the dark.

Once again, Geronimo took Top Dragster, with 9.70s at 144mph, beating Houndog. Dennis Priddle took out Pete Atkins' Slo-Mo-Shun for the Top Competition win, while Gerry Belton was back out in his Cobra taking Top Street.

The halcyon years of the sixties were over, and it marked an end of an era for British drag racing. New faces coming into the sport had differing views of how drag racing should be run in Britain, and a new club (the National Drag Racing Club) was formed to run meets at Santa Pod and other venues while a very heated AGM nearly saw the end of the BDR & HRA.

John Bennett left the sport at the end of the year and it was hoped that his enthusiasm and efforts to establish drag racing in Britain would be carried on by others as British drag racing moved into the seventies.

Published just before Christmas 1969, *Hot Car* magazine had the Malibu Express team as its front cover feature, boding well for the new decade. (Courtesy Mike Collins Archives)

This book showcases amazing machines and their riders in the ultimate acceleration sport – drag bike racing. Great photographs are combined with the author's in-depth knowledge, to explore, for the first time, the sport in the UK, and chart its relentless pursuit for ever more speed.

Paperback • 20.5x19cm • £14.99* UK / $29.95* US • 96 pages • 100 colour and b&w pictures • ISBN: 978-1-845843-14-4

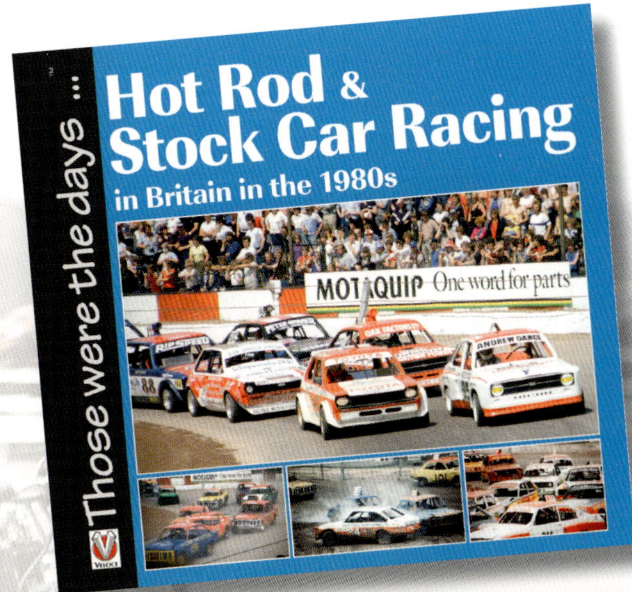

This book charts the development of short oval motor racing in the UK, using 100 never-before-published photographs. Championship listings complement the evocative text.

Paperback • 20.5x19cm • £12.99* UK / $25.95* US • 96 pages • 109 colour and b&w pictures • ISBN: 978-1-845841-67-6

For more info on Veloce titles, visit our website at www.veloce.co.uk
email info@veloce.co.uk • tel: +44 (0)1305 260068 • *prices subject to change • p+p extra

Also from Veloce:-

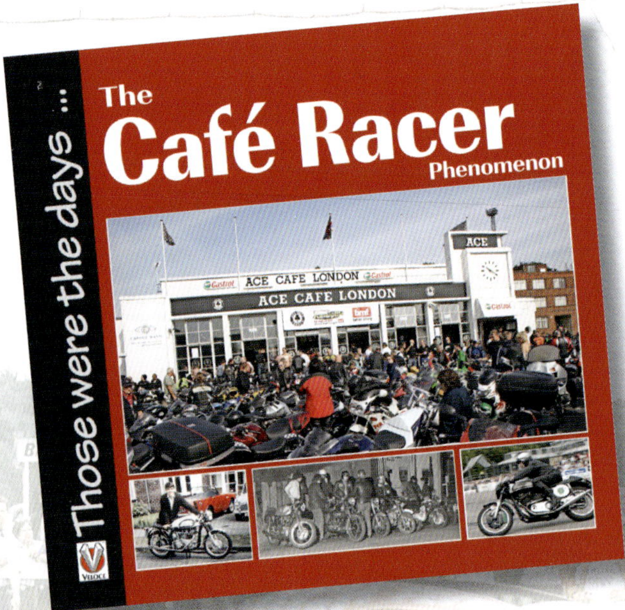

The Café Racer is one of the most enduring styles of motorcycle ever created, encapsulating the rebellious spirit of the 50s. Featuring a huge, global Café Racer directory alongside a unique mix of personal memories, previously unseen photos, iconic machines and chassis builders in profile, this book is a must for any 'ton-up' rider.

Paperback • 20.7x25cm • £14.99* UK / $29.95* US • 96 pages • 100 colour and b&w pictures • ISBN: 978-1-845842-64-2

Evocative pictures of British Touring Car racing – the crowd's favourite – from the flares of the late 1960s to the turbos of 1990. Features shots of all aspects of the racing – the drivers, the cars, the paddocks, and more.

Paperback • 20.5x19cm • £14.99* UK / $29.95* US • 96 pages • 100 colour and b&w pictures • ISBN: 978-1-845842-47-5

For more info on Veloce titles, visit our website at www.veloce.co.uk
email info@veloce.co.uk • tel: +44 (0)1305 260068 • *prices subject to change • p+p extra

INDEX